A Magical Fairytale for All
Elementary School Students

The Rise of a Math Genius

Written by :
Anho Jo

A Math Book that Your Child Can Solve on Their Own

Many parents wish for their children to enjoy math. It's not necessarily that they want their child to major in it. A parent worries that their child will struggle with studying mathematics. Perhaps you are looking at this book with the hope that your child will not find math difficult.

There are two things that are needed to enjoy math. The first is to strengthen a child's understanding of arithmetic operations and mathematical concepts, while the second is to learn with a positive mind. While learning operations and concepts is important, learning with a positive mindset is not easy. A child feels good during math when they solve a difficult math problem on their own or logically follow the steps of a problem. However, this book was not written to simply challenge the child with difficult problems, but to teach the basic principles of mathematics. The concepts will develop as the child completes each one logically.

All knowledge is divided into conceptual knowledge and procedural knowledge, and mathematics is no different. Teaching procedural knowledge, also known as technique, while expanding the knowledge aside from procedural knowledge is a principle. Therefore, while studying math, the child needs to understand both concepts and principles. This book focuses more on principles over concepts. Originally, this book is a fairy tale adaptation of my book, ' Fourth grade, Grab the Principles of Mathematics'('초등 4학년, 수학의 원리를 잡아라). It was a book for children and parents to study together, but the purpose of the adaptation is to adapt it to a fairy tale so that busy and overworking parents can rest and allow their children to read it alone.

This book is a children's book with a story, but the book is meant to focus more on the mathematical concepts rather than the story itself. Among the shapes, it only deals with 'length' by using logs and threads. If you understand the concept of 'length', you can develop the ability to operate numbers that can decompose, synthesize, and even manipulate. The next concept following 'length' is 'width,' and if the response of this book is good, I will write a second book describing 'width.' Errors and fun are hidden in the parts where mistakes are made and passed over while solving the problems of the principle. In this book, it is organized so that math can be more fun by capturing and easily connecting those 'small parts that are missed'. Although it is called a joy, the joy of math is more a subtle pleasure than a burst of joy. There's a paradox: "Parents make money for their children's self-made lives." It is the duty of parents and adults to provide the right tools, books and/or teachers for a child to be good at math. However, if you predict the child's level in math skills and just give the easy solution of the problem to the child by matching his/her skill, the child won't achieve any change. Once the child learns the concepts and principles of math, I hope you give enough time for your child to "step up to improve his or her skills." Even if there are some difficult parts, the parents should wait for their child to realize the mathematical principle by constantly repeating themselves.

I tried to organize the contents so that most elementary school students who are capable of receitng the multiplication table could understand it without difficulty. I hope that children read this book and think that math is not difficult, and that it is a familiar idea that always exists in and around our lives. I hope parents will put aside their fears of math for a while and enjoy reading this book alongside their children.

Sincerely,

Anho Jo
Author

Dear students

If Possible, Can You Solve the Problems Alone?

You may consider this book as a fairy tale book, but it's also a mathematical book. I hope you enjoy the story while improving your math skills.

I worked on this book while wondering, "How can I make understanding the principles of mathematics easier for the students?" Sometimes, however, there are problems where even 'I' can't explain easily. Math may seem easy or difficult on the outside, but if you take your time and look carefully, you will eventually be able to reach the answer.

If there's anything that's hard to understand, you can ask the adults or teachers around you, but I hope you can solve it on your own if you can. If you read this book with your parents, I would be very happy, but I hope you won't force your parents to do so because they are as busy and exhausted as you.

If any of you find difficulty in understanding fundamental arithmetic operations, I want you to train with an app called 〈조안호의 국민연산〉. Even if you read this book thoroughly and understand most of it, I would recommend reading it multiple times to understand better. Now, shall we dive in and have fun reading while solving the questions together?

Sincerely,

Anho Jo
Author

Who should read this book?

- All elementary students who learned the multiplication table
- Elementary school students who want to experience the principles of mathematics
- Upper-grade elementary school students who say math is not fun

Characters

Oreum Cha

A boy who likes to talk and play alone, who always sleeps during math class and has no choice but to go to school because his mom told him to go. After meeting Eunbi, he becomes a math genius.

Eunbi Cho

The youngest math genius recognized in the world. While helping Teacher Mole, a science teacher, she got involved in a dispute regarding mathematics and science. Eventually, she turned into a zombie. What should she do to get back to her original state?

Teacher Mole

As a science teacher, he spends every night in the laboratory studying, and his beard is shaggy and cranky. Because of this, students call him a mole.

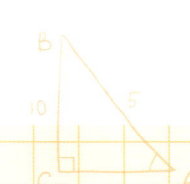

Table of Contents

Dear Parents   A Math Book that Your Child Can Solve on Their Own   **03**

Dear Students   If Possible, Can You Solve the Problems Alone?   **05**

Part 1. Tree Log   **10**

I Met a Math Zombie   13

My Deal with the Math Zombie   34

How Many Pieces?.   40

I Can Cut Several Logs at Once   58

Mom Signed Me Up for the Math Club   68

> Teacher Jo's Talk Talk   Cut and Leftover   73

Meeting Eunbi Again   74

How Much Remains After Cutting?   78

I Was Almost Late for the Math Club   84

> Teacher Jo's Talk Talk   It's Multiple Questions   88

> Special   What Would It Look Like If You Draw Like this?   89

Tree Logs of Different Sizes   90

The Rising Star of the Math Club   111

> Special   It Has An Interesting Shape   116

> Teacher Jo's Talk Talk   There Are Identical Tree Logs   117

Let's Change the Tree Log!   118

> Special   Did You Realize the Problems Are Identical to the Tree Log Problem?   138

Math Club: Still a Chill Vice President   139

Part 2. Can You Fold It? — 144

Teacher Jo's Talk Talk Let's Cut the Thread	146
Focus on How Many Times the Thread is Cut	147
Special Wrap the Thread Around the Scissors and Cut	163
Awaiting the Math Club	165
Special You Have to Solve with the Definition of Line Segment	169
Teacher Jo's Talk Talk Do You Know the Difference in Counting Numbers Starting at 0 and 1, Respectively?	170
Teacher Mole Knows My Name	171
Counting Numbers from One	179
Special Solve by a Definition of Counting	186
Counting from Zero	187
Oreum Even Solves Difficult Problems!	192
Special It's Not a Nonsense Problem	195
Teacher Jo's Talk Talk Fold the wire to Make the Shape	196
Finally Learning Shapes	197
Teaching Minseok	214
Special The Sheep Wants to be Free	218
Teacher Jo's Talk Talk How Many Stakes Are There?	219
Support with a Stake So That It didn't Line Up	220
Even Minseok Gets a Hundred	243
Special It's a Nostalgic Matchstick Problem	254
Answers	255

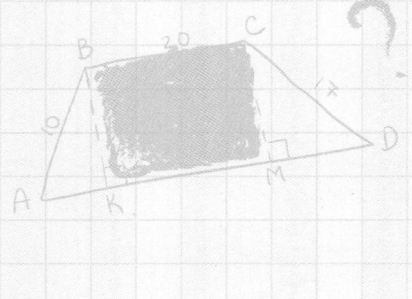

PART 1

Tree Log

I Met a Math Zombie

On a sunny spring day, the children cheered and ran outside carrying their bags. After all the children left, Oreum also carried his bag and left the classroom door.

As Oreum approached the playground, children were playing soccer. Oreum walked along the trails of the playground so that he wouldn't interfere with soccer, yet a soccer ball rolled towards Oreum. In the distance, Minseok gestured and shouted, "Hey, Oreum, pass the ball over." Oreum kicked the ball as hard as he could, but he stumbled as if he would fall and took several steps forward. His movements looked like a drunken man

stumbling. Minseok's friends were looking at Oreum while waiting for the soccer ball and laughing their heads off. Embarrassed, Oreum quickly grabbed the soccer ball and threw it towards Minseok as hard as he could. The soccer ball didn't even go half way to Minseok, but Minseok quickly ran and took the soccer ball.

Even from Oreum's point of view, Minseok is really good at soccer as well as running. However, Oreum is not envious of him whatsoever. He didn't understand why Minseok feels the need to run around so much.

Oreum loves walking. When he walked along the road and looked around, he notices that the world is full of unusual things. "Nobody has planted them, but since when did those flowers bloom like that again?" he thought to himself. The flowers nearby seem to be blooming more this year.

Oreum walked along the greater celandines ("yellow flowers") under the school playground wall. Then suddenly, he stopped walking and picked a celandine. A yellow liquid flowed out like yellow excrement between the cut yellow grass. Oreum stuck out his tongue and touched the liquid slightly with the tip of his tongue. The bitter and spicy taste seemed to paralyze the tongue, so Oreum quickly bent over, vomited, and continued spitting out the saliva in his mouth.

At that moment, Oreum remembered what his teacher said in science class.

"The greater celandine is a yellow flower with yellow liquid coming out of it, but the liquid is highly toxic, so you shouldn't eat it."

As Oreum remembered that, he spat and gagged even more. He thought to himself: 'I only put a little in my mouth, so nothing should happen, right?'

At that time, Minseok, who was resting while playing soccer, said to his friends, "Hey, Oreum is at it again." Minseok, who was sitting, stood up and shouted at Oreum, "Are you okay, Oreum?"

Oreum raised one hand to signal that he was okay and

ran so that his friends could not see him.

A while ago, the group of kids laughed because Oreum missed a soccer ball. Now they saw him gag from the taste of the flower. He felt embarrassed and he wanted to hide away somewhere.

After running for such a long time, Oreum spotted a billboard that said, "Danger: Do not approach." "What's this? Oh! This is the place the teacher told us not to go near because it's dangerous," Oreum said.

Oreum remembered his homeroom teacher's words last month during the school assembly: "Everyone, do you know there is a 'Cheonji Dongsan' behind the warehouse at the end of the science room? The hill is going to be replaced with a school cafeteria. Construction will start soon, so please don't go there."

Although Oreum planned to go back, he thought of his classmates who would still be playing soccer. He decided to wait until they are no longer around.

Building materials were already piled up, and wooden

pillars with red lines were also implanted here and there.

The nice-looking pine tree was circled with white paint.

Below the pine tree were the greater celandine flowers laying like a yellow carpet. It was amazing to find such a quiet and beautiful place in the middle of the town.

Although the spicy and bitter taste lingered in his mouth, he couldn't help but find the tiny flowers beautiful.

Oreum went to the science lab storage room to go up the 'Cheonji Dongsan.'

He said to himself, "The science teacher isn't here, is he?" as he looked around.

Oreum confirmed that no one was there. As he tried to go up to the narrow road next to the science room warehouse, he noticed another entrance behind the warehouse.

"What is that? Is it another warehouse?"

He hesitated and thought, "Should I just pass by? Or

should I go inside?

The door is open." Then, he thought, "It's going to just be a small peek. If I don't tell anyone, it should be fine, right?" He took one step towards the warehouse.

Oreum opened the door slightly and looked inside.

"Huh, there's a staircase that goes down." He saw a set of stairs that lead to a lower floor.

Oreum began to go down step by step. When he went down the stairs, he stepped into a large basement.

He was disappointed to see nothing matching his expectations. "It's just an empty basement…"

As soon as Oreum turned around to head back upstairs, he heard a rustling sound.

He started to get nervous as he heard it.

"Did I perhaps hear wrong?" Oreum wondered as he carefully scanned the warehouse. Then, he saw a moving black object.

Oreum wanted to scream and run away, but he couldn't speak nor move an inch.

He couldn't do anything but stay still on the spot.

The black object slowly approached Oreum, who eventually collapsed out of fear. He was so scared that he shuddered all over and closed his eyes.

He closed eyes for a while, but nothing happened.

Oreum summoned a bit of courage to open his eyes. The black object was standing right in front of Oreum while staring. However, an iron bar cage was standing between the two. Oreum was relieved to think the black object wouldn't approach any further.

After taking a step back, he looked closely at the black object. As the black object no longer moved, Oreum's urge to leave only grew stronger.

Oreum turned around and walked slowly when the black object finally spoke:

"Kid, are you going to leave just like that?"

As the object spoke those words, Oreum once again collapsed on the floor.

Oreum eventually asked with a trembling voice, "Ah, so you can speak! Who, who are you?"

The object said in a quiet voice, "…looks tasty."
"What did you say?" Oreum asked. The black object replied in surprise, "I … didn't say anything."
"My name is Eunbi Cho." the object said right after with a pretty girl's voice. Hearing the voice, he felt more relieved. Oreum's fear disappeared at once.

Oreum became more curious after learning that the black object was a girl of the same age as him.
"Why are you here?" he asked.
"Hmm… it would be hard to believe, but…"
Eunbi lowered her head with shame and spoke in a quiet voice.
"I'm… not human."

Oreum was curious rather than scared.
"If you're not human, then what are you? A ghost? A

goblin?"

Eunbi shook her head.

Oreum continued to ask with curiosity and a slightly joking manner.

"Then, a zombie?"

Hoping that Oreum wouldn't be scared after knowing her identity,

Eunbi replied, "Yeah, I'm a zombie."

"Hahaha~" Oreum laughed for a while as he heard the absurd statement and said, "You're joking, right? Zombies and ghosts only show on TV."

However, as Oreum gradually got used to the darkness, he began to see Eunbi little by little.

Only then did Oreum see that Eunbi looked a little strange. Even in the dark, her face looked too white.

"Now you know that I look weird. To tell you the truth, my heart can't make blood." Eunbi lowered her head with dejection.

"How did you end up like this?" As Oreum asked, Eunbi began to explain things slowly.

"I used to be a math genius. No, people always called me a math genius. Even mathematicians around the world wanted to meet me."

"Wow, that sounds cool! I don't like math."

"Why do you hate math? Math is something that anyone can do easily." Eunbi said.

"That's what people who are good at math say," said Oreum sourly.

"But why are you stuck in a place like this?"

"It's because of my science teacher."

"You mean Teacher Mole?"

Oreum recalled the science teacher.

Like a person who came from a tunnel in the ground, the teacher's hair looks like it hasn't been washed for days, and his beard is bushy. He also wears the same clothes everyday. Because of this, all the kids call him Teacher Mole.

With that, Oreum was curious as to how Teacher Mole was related to the incident.

"What did Teacher Mole do?"

"He looked down at the mathematicians and called them all idiots."

"What do you mean?" Oreum couldn't understand what Eunbi meant by that.

Oreum thought that Eunbi wanted to defend the mathematicians since she is a math genius herself, but Oreum decided to listen more to Eunbi's story.

"So what happened next?" Oreum asked, begging to know the remaining parts of the story.

"Science isn't absolute, so there are times when new theories often refute past theories. But mathematics is more of a complete discipline for mathematicians to create eternal things, which are concepts. I told the teacher that math can be done by anyone because of that reason. The teacher heard this and was angry. He thought that I didn't respect scientists at all. He said to me, 'Can all math problems really be solved with concepts ?' I said yes afterwards. He told me to prove it. Before I knew it, he gave me an injection that turned me into a zombie."

Although Oreum couldn't understand the whole thing, he could imagine the cranky teacher doing something like that.

"Yeah, Teacher Mole is always inspired by new discoveries. When his students don't think the same, he calls them ignorant and doesn't treat them like humans. He thinks he is the smartest and brightest in the world."

Oreum said.

Hearing Oreum, Eunbi answered, "The teacher did say he's researching something important and the whole world will be amazed. He said he needed my help, so I

participated in it." Eunbi seemed to regret her decision.

Oreum listened with growing curiosity

"And then?"

"When the research reached its end, we argued. He then injected me with the test fluid," Eunbi sobbed as she was looking at her white hands.

Oreum was baffled. "So his 'great research study' was turning people into zombies?"

"Well, the teacher's research was great. Nobody knows yet how to freeze a man for years, get his blood back to normal, and make his heart beat again. That's why he wanted to turn humans into zombies to get rid of all the blood. He is experimenting on how to get the heart of zombies to beat again," Eunbi spoke in awe of Teacher Mole's research.

"Wow, did Teacher Mole do that kind of research? Did he also make the cure to turn you back to normal?" Oreum asked.

Eunbi closed her eyes and said, "I'm not sure. The

research has reached its final stage, but I don't know if it's done… He did make me like this after all."

Oreum said with worry, "Then there is a chance you will be a zombie forever."

"Last week, the teacher was excited that he brought a bottle and boasted that he succeeded in the experiment. Then he told me that I needed to prove my words if I wanted to leave. I think it's true that he succeeded in the research."

"That's a relief. At least you can turn back into a human," Oreum said.

"That's right. I told the teacher that if you learn the concepts well, all children can become math geniuses. I still believe that it's true, and I trust myself," Eunbi exclaimed confidently.

Oreum was reassured after hearing Eunbi's story.

However, Eunbi's face was filled with worry. "What's wrong? Let's prove the teacher and leave this place. Don't you want to go back home?" Oreum urged.

"I want to. But I can't leave looking like this. And I might gnaw on the people outside. Even now, I want to bite you and suck your blood."

It was hard to see because she was all white, but Eunbi seemed to move her mouth.

"Ah! What was that sound?" Oreum said in shock as he curled his body.

"I told you, I'm a zombie," Eunbi replied with a distressed face.

Oreum took a step back in fear.

"There's nothing to be scared of. Don't worry. I can't go near you because of these iron bars."

In discomfort, Eunbi matched the pace of her neck and shoulders, leaning on one side.

Oreum, who saw Eunbi suffering, was scared, but also felt sorry for her.

Eunbi straightened herself and said to Oreum with a pitiful voice, "I need your help. You said you're not good with math, right?" "Yeah. Math makes my head hurt, and I hate math the most."

Eunbi spoke to Oreum with hope, "Then I can help you become a math genius. Trust me."

"No thanks. I don't want to be a math genius. I want to stay like this. I should go now, I've been here for too long."

Oreum turned around to leave.

"Wait! Please help me. You have been the only person to come here after all this time." Eunbi pleaded desperately.

However, Oreum replied sternly, "No. Thinking about math makes my head explode. I don't get why people do math anyway."

With determination, Eunbi said in a firm voice, "Then

I have no choice but to speak." Oreum stopped to ask anxiously, "What are you going to say?"

"I'm telling the teacher that you came down here. Then you won't be able to live like you are now. He might turn you into a zombie and you will have to stay down here with me."

Eunbi talked as if she was relaxed.

Oreum suddenly felt a chill in his spine.

He stopped walking and didn't know what to do.

Oreum was terrified thinking that Teacher Mole will turn him into a zombie and lock him in the dark warehouse. Oreum regretted coming down here, but there was no turning back.

My Deal with the Math Zombie

Oreum approached Eunbi slowly.

"What do I have to do? Will I really become a genius like you say?"

Eunbi continued to talk with a desperate heart to persuade Oreum.

"Yes. You should believe me. Math isn't hard at all," she said with confidence.

"But just looking at the numbers gives me a headache and makes me sleepy!" Oreum exclaimed with suspicion in his expression.

Eunbi was confused. "How can you sleep while doing math? It's fun."

"It's not just me. Minseok sleeps, my seat partner doodles during class, and our class president only memorizes English vocabulary."

Eunbi lowered her head hearing this and murmured, "I see. That's why the science teacher was so mad."

"What did Teacher Mole say?" Oreum asked.

"He said the kids don't like math, so he told me that the people teaching math should reflect on themselves."

Oreum nodded while saying, "That's true."

Eunbi continued, "I don't know why you guys came to hate math so much."

"It's because I don't understand anything. I don't get why we have to learn math either."

Eunbi made a sad face at Oreum's words.

"But anyone can do math. Mathematicians already

created the concepts. We're just using the concepts to solve the problems, as if we're using silverware to eat our food." As Eunbi spoke in frustration, Oreum shouted with an annoyed voice. "I know that! It's still too hard!"

Eunbi immediately refuted. "It's not hard. It's because it's not taught properly. Do you play computer games?"

Oreum was intrigued by the words 'computer games.' "Yeah. Who doesn't play computer games? My classmates can play all night." Eunbi saw Oreum and claimed, "Computer games are also created by someone. Rules are also decided. You all follow those rules and play the games. Math is the same. It's created like computer games, and rules are decided."

"But with math, you have to calculate large numbers…" Oreum replied with a quiet voice. He fiddled with his fingers, embarrassed that he couldn't calculate.

Eunbi comforted Oreum by answering, "You don't need to calculate the large ones. Those problems don't appear

often even in secondary school. You just need to be able to calculate small numbers well."

Oreum said as if he were trying to keep his pride, "Well, I can calculate the small numbers…"

"Math isn't just about calculation. Thinking logically is also important. If you connect your thoughts one by one, you'll be surprised how fun math is."

"…Really?" Oreum seemed to be convinced by Eunbi's words.

Oreum was starting to believe the words of the math genius standing in front of him.

Above all, he wanted to get Eunbi out of the dark basement somehow.

"Yes, I will teach you the path to become a math genius," Eunbi said.

"Okay. What am I supposed to do?"

Seeing that Oreum was persuaded, Eunbi beamed with delight.

"First, you need to follow what I say. Shall we start right now?" Eunbi was worried that Oreum would change his mind, so she wanted to start right away. However, Oreum said as he turned around, "It's too late today. I have to go now. I'm sure my mom will be worried."

"Okay, but don't forget. You have to come back here after class tomorrow!" Eunbi continued to confirm multiple times, worried that Oreum wouldn't return.

Oreum felt burdened with weight on his shoulders.

"Got it." Oreum finally left the basement and saw the sun setting outside. As he had come to his senses, he suddenly started running. He didn't realize that he had been talking with Eunbi for this long.

Thinking of his mother, Oreum ran even faster. After arriving home, he greeted his mother nonchalantly and entered his room. Oreum's thoughts were so filled with Eunbi that he couldn't hear his mother nagging.

How Many Pieces?

The next day, unlike other days, Oreum carried his bag as soon as the bell rang and went to the warehouse where Eunbi was waiting. No one in the class seemed to notice Oreum's absence.

When Oreum arrived, he saw Eunbi crouching in the corner and making a low but grotesque sound.

"I'm here," he called out. He was scared of the sound, but he did his best to reach out to her in a bright tone. Eunbi saw Oreum and straightened herself up. Smiling, she touched her face and said, "You came after all. I was worried you wouldn't come back here."

Nodding, Oreum said, "I made a promise. You need to promise, too. Don't tell the teacher even though I don't become a math genius as you say, okay?" Eunbi heard this and responded with a confident smile.

"Don't worry. You will become a math genius from my teaching. If by any chance you don't, I will keep my promise."

Although Oreum was a little relieved, his anxiety remained.

"Then, shall we start?" Oreum's heart began to beat at the anticipation of his first day.

Oreum was still reluctant to study math. Eunbi noticed Oreum's feelings and picked up a tree log.

"What are you doing with a log?" Seeing the tree log, Oreum was puzzled.

Eunbi changed her attitude and asked in a slightly dull tone.

"There is one tree log. How many pieces are there when you cut it?"

Oreum laughed. "Are you kidding me? Even babies would know this." With a frown, Eunbi said, "Just answer my question." With disapproval, Oreum said,

(1) "☐ pieces."

"Correct."

"There is one tree log. How many pieces are there when you cut it twice so that it doesn't overlap?"

(2) "☐ pieces."

"There is one tree log. How many pieces are there when you cut it three times so that it doesn't overlap?"

(3) "☐ pieces."

Eunbi started asking questions at a faster pace.

"There is one tree log. How many pieces are there when you cut it four times so that it doesn't overlap?"

(4) " ☐ pieces."

"There is one tree log. How many pieces are there when you cut it five times so that it doesn't overlap?"

(5) " ☐ pieces."

"There is one tree log. How many pieces are there when you cut it six times so that it doesn't overlap?"

(6) " ☐ pieces."

"There is one tree log. How many pieces are there when you cut it seven times so that it doesn't overlap?"

(7) " ☐ pieces."

"That's enough. Are you fooling around?" Oreum thought that the problems are way too easy so far.

"It's easy right? So did you find the rule?"

"Rule? What rule?" Oreum asked in a dumbfounded expression.

"What's that all about? Then you should've told me to find the rule in the first place."

Eunbi answered, trying to calm Oreum down,

"Sorry about that. Calm down and think about the rule behind these problems."

"I did answer the problems, but I think it's hard to explain how I answered them."

Eunbi saw Oreum glancing with hesitance and took out a blackboard.

"Look at this graph and think of the blank spaces." Oreum observed the graph carefully and exclaimed proudly, "I figured it out!"

"Hmph, that was nothing. I knew it the whole time. You confused me by explaining rules in a difficult way." Oreum turned his head with a pout.

Ignoring Oreum's pouting, Eunbi moved on.

"So you understand the rule that there is one more piece of log over the number of times it is cut, right? You got it, right?"

Oreum's anger grew from Eunbi's words.

"I told you I got it! What do you even see me as?"

Smiling, Eunbi said, "Now I'm going to cut it multiple times."

"Cut however much you want," Oreum said with confidence, but he was secretly nervous.

"There is one tree log. How many pieces are there when you cut it a hundred times so that it doesn't overlap?"

(9) "☐ pieces."

"No matter how many times I cut the log, you just need to use that number and apply to the rule. You don't need to think hard on this."

"There is one tree log. How many pieces are there when you cut it seven-hundred ninety times so that it doesn't overlap?"

(10) "☐ pieces."

Eunbi gave Oreum a compliment: "Wow! You're getting the hang of solving."

Oreum felt proud after hearing a compliment, but couldn't help but remain nervous.

"So you can solve these problems even with large numbers, right? Now I'll change the question."

Oreum perked his ears up and listened attentively.

"There is one tree log. To make two pieces, how many times do you need to cut it?"

(11) "☐ time(s)."

"There is one tree log. To make three pieces, how many times do you need to cut it?"

(12) "☐ time(s)."

"There is one tree log. To make four pieces, how many times do you need to cut it?"

(13) "☐ time(s)."

"There is one tree log. To make five pieces, how many times do you need to cut it?"

(14) "☐ time(s)."

"There is one tree log. To make six pieces, how many times do you need to cut it?"

(15) "☐ time(s)."

"There is one tree log. To make seven pieces, how many times do you need to cut it?"

(16) "☐ time(s)."

"Did you find the rule?"

Oreum stayed motionlessly.

"You haven't found it yet?"

"No, I did. Give me the blackboard, I'll do it."

Oreum took the blackboard and filled in the blanks.

As Oreum continued to write the rule, Eunbi nodded, with a smile. "How is it? I got it correct, right?" Oreum asked with a grin.

"Yes, good job! See? It's not too hard." Eunbi emphasized once again that her words were correct.

Oreum then asked, "But these problems were easy to solve since they're simple. Aren't the problems going to get more difficult?" Oreum understands the school teacher's lectures, but seeing applied math problems makes his mind blank. With that, Oreum was still worried.

Eunbi didn't notice Oreum's worries and moved onto the next question. "Since you understand the problems so far, shall we practice these questions with the concept of multiplication added to them?"

"Wait, what? We're applying multiplication all of a sudden?"

"Why? Is there a problem?" Eunbi asked in wonder.

"I'm terrified of multiplication."

"Did you perhaps not memorize your multiplication tables?"

"What do you see me as? I'm good with multiplication tables. I even practiced by working backwards," Oreum said proudly.

"Then there should be no issues. If you just know the multiplication tables, it'll be easy." Eunbi immediately moved on to the next question.

> "There is one tree log. You are about to make two pieces, but it takes 4 minutes to cut the log once. How many minutes does it take to make two pieces?"
>
> (18) "☐ minutes."

Oreum was confused. "This doesn't seem like a multiplication problem. Did you say something wrong?"

"I know what I'm talking about. Just listen to the questions and answer them," Eunbi rebuked.

Tilting his head, Oreum responded, "Okay, keep them going!"

"There is one tree log. You are about to make three pieces, but it takes 4 minutes to cut the log once. How many minutes does it take to make three pieces?"

(19) "... ☐ minutes?"

Oreum answered hesitantly, worried that his answer was wrong.

"That's correct. Say it confidently. Why are you nervous?"

"Okay," Oreum replied. He gained some courage again after thinking to himself, "So what if I get them wrong? It's not like I'm solving test questions."

"There is one tree log. You are about to make four pieces, but it takes 4 minutes to cut the log once. How many minutes does it take to make four pieces?"

(20) "☐ minutes."

"Good job. Answer the questions with that confidence." Eunbi did her best to encourage Oreum.

"There is one tree log. You are about to make five pieces, but it takes 4 minutes to cut the log once. How many minutes did it take to make five pieces?"

(21) "☐ minutes."

"There is one tree log. You are about to make six pieces, but it takes 4 minutes to cut the log once. How many minutes does it take to make six pieces?"

(22) "☐ minutes."

"You're doing very well. See? You need to believe in yourself. Did you understand that the time to cut the log increases after each cut?"

Oreum nodded.

"Then 'adding the same number' can be turned into multiplication, right?"

"Then it should be easier to solve the problem, right?"

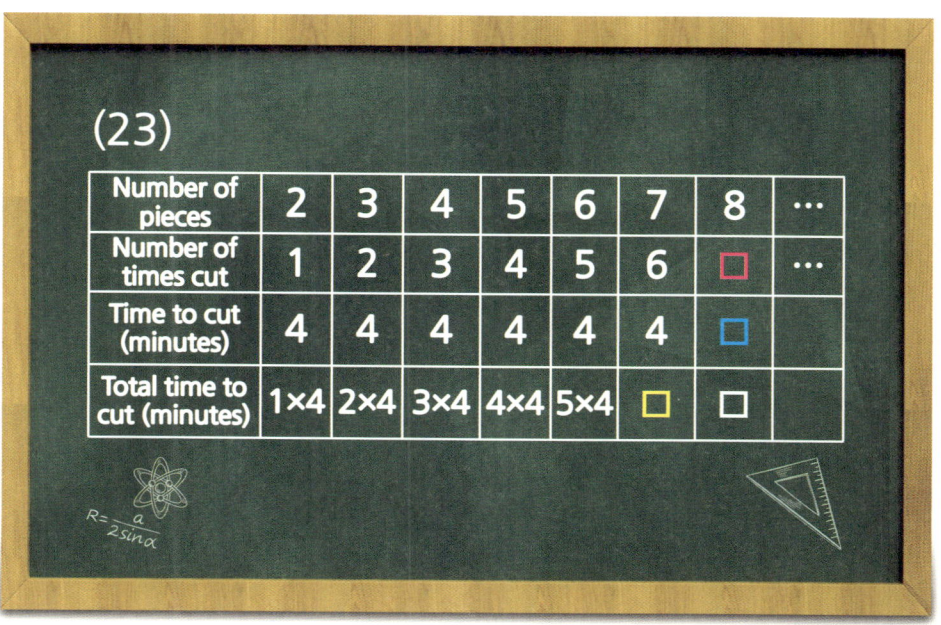

Strikingly, Oreum was able to understand the concepts.

"Yes, I think I can do it."

"I knew it. I told you you can do it. Now take a look at this graph. Fill the blanks in and find the rule."

Excited, Oreum examined the graph and started to fill in the blanks. After filling them out, Oreum looked up at Eunbi.

"How did I do?"

Eunbi smiled, saying "Great job!"

"Then, shall we move on to slightly more difficult problems?"

Although Oreum was nervous, he didn't lose his courage.

"There is one tree log. It takes 5 minutes to cut the log. Every time you cut, you need to rest for 2 minutes. If you plan to cut the log into eight pieces without overlapping, how many minutes will it take, including the final resting time?"

Oreum couldn't answer immediately this time. However, he then shouted,

(24) "I got it. ☐ minutes" with a loud voice.

Eunbi applauded. "That's it. You solved it well."

"You knew that it takes a total of 7 minutes to cut the log, including rest time. Just thinking a little will help you reach the answer."

Seeing that Oreum was following well, Eunbi decided to add something interesting.

"For this next problem, I put a trap. Try answering this one without falling for it" Eunbi said with a mysterious smile.

Oreum became tense after hearing this.

Eunbi looked at Oreum and tried to hold her laughter.

"There is one tree log. It takes 5 minutes to cut the log. Every time you cut, you need to rest for 2 minutes. If you plan to cut the log into eight pieces without overlapping, how many minutes will it take?"

"Isn't it the same question? 49 minutes."

"Incorrect. Think carefully. This problem isn't the same."

(25) "Ah, I got it now. ☐ minutes."

"It was a hard question, but you got it! I'm glad that you went past the trap! There is no need to add the 2 minutes to the last time you cut the log, right? This can actually be solved by anyone, but I think people don't solve it either because they think it's hard or their parents don't give enough time."

Although Oreum solved the problem, Eunbi felt more bad for the kids who found math difficult.

"I had fun solving these tree log problems more than I thought. Give me another problem."

Oreum felt happiness from solving a hard problem and he wanted to feel this joy again.

"Seeing you happy makes me want to give you another problem. But I think we should stop here. Instead, study what we went through a few times. That is your homework."

"Jeez, my math teacher at school gave a load of homework, but this math teacher in front of me didn't give me a problem when I ask for one."

Surprised that Eunbi ends her session so quickly, Oreum said sarcastically,

"Do you really think you can turn me into a math genius by giving me these math problems?"

Eunbi asked, "Oreum, do you think I became a math genius by solving a bunch of problems?"

"Rather than that, isn't it because you're just smart?" Oreum believed that only smart people can be good at math

"I feel so wronged. I put in a lot of effort to become the genius I am now, but people only say that I am born smart," Eunbi said, hoping to show Oreum that anyone can work hard to be skilled in math.

"To learn math, it is not important to just solve many problems. Instead, one should understand one concept or principle clearly and build up one by one to be good at math." Leaving behind Eunbi's seemingly unknown words, Oreum slowly headed home.

I Can Cut Several Logs at Once

When Oreum returned home, he thought in his head about cutting everything he could, such as pillars and chopsticks. Although it wasn't intentional, he couldn't stop thinking about the homework and tried to create his own math problems. He thought of the relation between the number of cuts and the number of pieces made by cutting, in addition to the cutting time, the resting time, etc. The next day, he ran to Eunbi after class. No one seemed to be curious where Oreum headed off to.

Eunbi had nothing else to do, so she was thinking of Oreum while waiting for him to come. "Welcome back. Let's now move on to questions about cutting multiple logs at once!"

"There are two tree logs. They are thin enough for you to cut them both at the same time. If you cut both logs at once, how many pieces are there?"

(26) " ☐ pieces."

Oreum answered without hesitation.

"You understand up to here, right? But cutting multiple times can cause confusion. If you just remember that the number increases by two everytime you cut, it'll be easier," Eunbi explained.

"Okay, I won't forget."

"There are two tree logs. They are thin enough for you to cut them both at the same time. If you cut both logs at once two times, how many pieces are there?"

(27) "That's easy. ☐ pieces."

"There are two tree logs. They are thin enough for you to cut them both at the same time. If you cut both logs at once three times, how many pieces are there?"

(28) "☐ pieces."

"There are two tree logs. They are thin enough for you to cut them both at the same time. If you cut both logs at once four times, how many pieces are there?"

(29) "☐ pieces."

"There are two tree logs. They are thin enough for you to cut them both at the same time. If you cut both logs at once five times, how many pieces are there?"

(30) "☐ pieces."

"Did you figure out the rule?" Eunbi observed Oreum's expression.

"So you didn't find it yet. Try figuring it out while filling in the blanks."

Eunbi then gave Oreum the blackboard with a graph.

Oreum filled in each black on the graph while trying to find the rule behind the problems

"Shall we move on to the next problem?" Eunbi asked. Oreum nodded his head.

"Yes, I found the rule," Oreum answered while staring at the graph. If Oreum saw this problem before he met Eunbi, he would've remained confused. He was just amazed at how easy the math problems looked now.

While Oreum was lost in thought, Eunbi prepared another problem.

"Oreum, do you want to stop?" Oreum came to his senses and turned his head towards Eunbi.

"No, keep going. My mind has been changing, so I was amazed."

Smiling, Eunbi said, "Okay. Listen carefully to this problem."

Oreum wanted to listen to Eunbi's problem in more detail, so he turned his head slightly to the side.

"There are three tree logs. They are thin enough for you to cut them all at the same time. If you cut all the logs at once, how many pieces are there?"

(32) "☐ pieces."

"Good..It's easy to think first about the number of pieces made each time one log is cut. In other words, when you cut once, you can triple the amount of pieces made. How about it? Do you think you can do it?" Oreum then answered with a tone brighter than yesterday.

"Yes, I can. This is really fun." Oreum waited in excitement for the next set of problems.

"There are three tree logs. They are thin enough for you to cut them all at the same time. If you cut all the logs at once two times, how many pieces are there?"

(33) "☐ pieces."

"There are three tree logs. They are thin enough for you to cut them all at the same time. If you cut all the logs at once three times, how many pieces are there?"

(34) "☐ pieces."

"There are three tree logs. They are thin enough for you to cut them all at the same time. If you cut all the logs at once four times, how many pieces are there?"

(35) "□ pieces."

"There are three tree logs. They are thin enough for you to cut them all at the same time. If you cut all the logs at once five times, how many pieces are there?"

(36) "□ pieces."

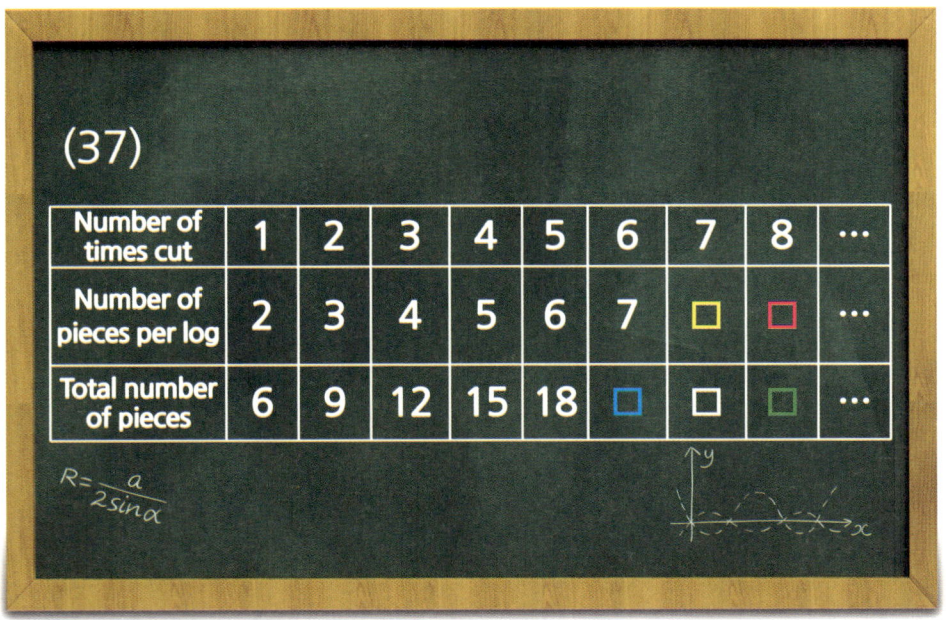

(37)

Number of times cut	1	2	3	4	5	6	7	8	...
Number of pieces per log	2	3	4	5	6	7	□	□	...
Total number of pieces	6	9	12	15	18	□	□	□	...

"Yes, very good. Did you find the rule?"

Oreum is still not used to figuring out the rules. Oreum was about to think of something silently, but Eunbi didn't give him any time to think.

"Look at this graph. Find the rule by filling in the blanks."

Oreum could've found the rule on his own if he was given just a little more time, but he found Eunbi a bit cheeky for not waiting for him, so he snatched the blackboard off her hands.

Eunbi looked at Oreum and said,

"Aren't the problems similar to multiplication tables? Once you find the rule, you can solve the problems with even larger numbers, right?"

Oreum didn't say anything.

"There are four fine sticks. They are thin enough for you to cut them all at the same time. If you cut all the sticks at once five times, how many pieces are there?"

(38) "☐ pieces." Oreum answered bluntly.

"There are five fine sticks. They are thin enough for you to cut all five at the same time. In order to make 40 pieces, how many times do you need to cut all the sticks at a time?"

(39) "☐ pieces."

Oreum answered without confusing himself.

Eunbi asked the questions cautiously as Oreum seemed angry.

"There are times when one gets confused while solving these problems, so let's solve together."

"This time, let's change the rules. After cutting one stick, let us use a rule where you re-cut the two pieces made at the same time. Using this rule, **if you cut the two sticks three times, how many pieces are there?**"

Oreum read the questions twice and answered,

(40) "☐ pieces."

He then said quietly while standing up, "I think I have to go."

Eunbi was troubled that Oreum couldn't get over his anger, but there was nothing else she could do.

"Okay, you understood the solution, $2\times2\times2\times2$, right? You look tired, so take a rest. I'll see you tomorrow." Eunbi was afraid that Oreum wouldn't come back.

Oreum answered with, "I have an afternoon club tomorrow. I'll come the day after" and left the warehouse.

Oreum felt strange. He felt like his heart was pounding with excitement while solving the problems. He didn't seem like he was himself at the moment. He felt ashamed and embarrassed of the days he took naps during class, but that wasn't all he felt. He felt that something else had awakened inside. It' was a feeling that Oreum didn't want to forget. It' was as if he had been in the dark for a long time only to come out and greet the beautiful and mystical world.

Mom Signed Me Up for the Math Club

Oreum couldn't go see Eunbi after class right away these days. This was because his mom had added the after-school math club to his schedule without his permission, hoping that Oreum would work harder on math.

When Oreum asked in anger why she added him to the math club without his permission, she replied by saying that she didn't want him to become someone who gave up on math like she did. Oreum usually didn't do anything good to his mother, so he did his best to understand.

So today, Oreum came to do math club activities after class. It was an unfamiliar area for him since it was his first day, and he was nervous because he came to do math, which was a subject he usually wasn't good at. Oreum went to an empty seat and sat quietly. Each student arrived and sat down.

The children greeted each other. Not one student went up to greet Oreum. Just then, the vice president came in. The vice president looked around to find himself a seat. He looked at the empty seat next to Oreum, looked coy and sat down without saying hello. He took out his pencil case and a practice book from his backpack and put it on his desk. The vice president looked at Oreum, but didn't act like they know him. Instead, he just looked at their own sources.

At that time, a sixth-grader wearing thick glasses frames was writing something on the blackboard. After writing, he faced the students and said, "I wrote a math problem on the board. I want each of you to try and answer it. After that, discuss among yourselves. In addition, make a similar type of problem and give it to your friends. I will come back in an hour to tell you the answer."

The sixth-grader came down from the platform and opened the front door of the classroom to leave.

As soon as the sixth-grader left, the vice president next to Oreum solved the problem without hesitation in the practice book. While some students went on to solve the problem, others just fooled around without looking at the problem. Oreum read the problem and thought.

'Why would the mother in this problem want to grill the toast in 9 minutes? Moms create problems we don't have to do to annoy us.' Oreum thought of his mother who nags him for nothing. Then, he thought of Eunbi, who was still locked in the warehouse as a zombie.

"If it was Eunbi, she would've solved the problem without too much thought," Oreum murmured to himself while reading the problem again.

You are about to cook 3 pieces of toast. You can only grill two pieces of toast at once and you need to cook both sides of the toast. Each side takes 3 minutes to cook. It would take 6 minutes to cook the first two pieces of toast and another 6 minutes to cook the last piece of toast, but the mother apparently grilled all three pieces in nine minutes. Label each toast as A, B, and C and explain how she did it.

(41)

After solving the problem, Oreum couldn't help but smile.

He felt really proud. He glanced at the vice president next to him with pride. The vice president already solved the problem and was working on other problems. Although no one took interest in Oreum, he found the club not too bad.

| Teacher Jo's Talk Talk | # Cut and Leftover |

You can cut a given log and get what's left over by subtraction. Of course, you are extending on the idea of subtraction. By the way, I gave the definition of division as "a symbol of repeated subtraction." Did you know that? If not, don't delay and memorize right now. Math is about solving problems with definitions or concepts.

For example, **13-3-3-3-3=1** can be simplified using division into the equation. It becomes **13/3=4 R1**. If you flip it around, you get **3×4 + 1 = 13**. Although you learn this in 3rd grade, you'll go through this and expand your idea of multiples and divisors.

You can solve a problem related to this idea. For example, **'There is a 75 cm tree log. If you cut it into 7cm pieces without leaving anything out, how much is left over in cm?'** If you take the 75 cm log and cut it into ten (10) pieces of 7 cm, you get 5cm remaining. The equation becomes **75-7-7-7-7-7-7-7-7-7-7=5.** Change it into division and you get **75/7=10 R5.** If you subtract five from the original 75, you can get **(75-5)/7=10.** If you apply multiplication to this equation, you can get **75 - 5 = 7×10**.

It may be hard to understand right away because the equation keeps changing. However, things will be easier to memorize as long as the child knows that **'subtracting the remainder first will help divide equally.'** The divided number is not the divisor, but the multiple. Many 5th graders get confused by this. This is a part that many students find difficult, and here we study right up to the previous step.

Meeting Eunbi Again

Oreum hurriedly ran down the stairs of the warehouse to brag to Eunbi that he solved the problem from the math club. He saw Eunbi rubbing her face close to the iron bars. "Have you waited for me?" Oreum asked while smiling.

Eunbi answered with surprise, "N-No, I was just moving instinctively because I'm starving for blood. Sorry about that."

"Eunbi, are you that urgent for blood? Should I find some for you?"

Oreum was worried that Eunbi would bite him if she got released from the iron bars. On the other hand, he felt sorry for her.

"It's okay. If I drink blood now, I'll become even more dangerous. Thanks for worrying about me, Oreum."

Oreum wanted to tell Eunbi about what happened during the math club, but he stayed silent.

"I'm trying to hold it in, but my body moved on its own whenever I see you,"

Eunbi said as she turned around and slowly headed toward the walls.

At first, Oreum thought Eunbi was just going to prepare to teach math. However, she was facing the wall as she bent her whole body and screamed with aggressive and grotesque sounds as if she had strange symptoms. Oreum just sat down in place in fear. After Eunbi kept staggering and bending for a while, she covered her face. She looked like she was suffering greatly.

Eunbi looked up slowly, seemingly looking better. She then turned around and lumbered toward Oreum. Her face was even more pale than before, making her face apparently more white. Oreum felt more worried for Eunbi than scared. He thought of what would happen if Eunbi couldn't change back due to a strange symptom.

Oreum opened his mouth first.

"Are you okay?"

Eunbi was grateful for Oreum, who worried for her without being afraid.

"Yeah. Were you surprised?" Eunbi was rather worried that Oreum was surprised to see her behavior.

"I was. But I was worried."

"Don't worry too much. It was just a muscle spasm," Eunbi responded, pretending that nothing had happened. Although Oreum was worried, he saw Eunbi's calm expression and felt relieved.

"Shall we start now?"

Eunbi glanced at Oreum and picked up the tree log sitting next to her. "Let's take this log and move on to more fun problems." Eunbi took one among several tree logs and began her explanation.

Oreum still got anxious when the topic of math got brought up, but he calmed down and looked at Eunbi, who was still holding on to the tree log.

How Much Remains After Cutting?

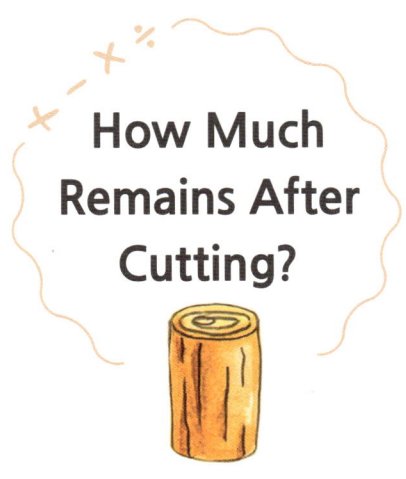

"There is one 60 cm long tree log. You cut 20 cm of the log. How many cm are left?"

(42) "☐ cm."

Oreum answered, thinking to himself relieved, 'Today's questions aren't too difficult.'

"This problem wasn't too difficult to solve, right? You will be able to solve today's math problems." Eunbi said, seemingly as she had read Oreum's mind.

Oreum nodded, but he didn't lose his focus

"There is one 60 cm long tree log. If you cut the log into two equal pieces, how long is one piece in cm?"

(43) "☐ cm."

"There is one 60 cm long tree log. If you cut the log into three equal pieces, how long is one piece in cm?"

(44) "☐ cm."

"There is one 60 cm long tree log. If you cut the log into four equal pieces, how long is one piece in cm?"

Oreum seemed to be lost in thought for a moment, but then he took the blackboard and wrote something. Eunbi waited for him. After solving, Oreum answered with a confident tone,

(45) "☐ cm."

"Very good. It's important that you could calculate the solution," Eunbi said, complimenting him. Eunbi continued with the rally of questions.

"There is one 60 cm long tree log. If you cut the log into five equal pieces, how long is one piece in cm?"

(46) "☐ cm." Oreum answered while calculating the answer on the blackboard.

"There is one 60 cm long tree log. If you cut the log into six equal pieces, how long is one piece in cm?"

(47) "☐ cm."

After answering, Oreum looked at the blackboard. It was now full of handwritten work. He erased the board and perked his ears at Eunbi's voice.

"I arranged 12 identical stones in a line. After placing a thread on top of the stones, the thread measures out to be 12 cm. How many cm is one stone?"

"Wait, it's not a tree log problem? Give me a log problem. It's confusing," Oreum said with frustration. He was surprised to receive a stone problem all of a sudden.

"Don't think too much about the tree log or the stone. Listen to the problem carefully and think of what it asks for. Gosh, you're being nitpicky on everything," Eunbi remarked, dumbfounded.

Oreum didnn't say anything, knowing that Eunbi hadn't said anything wrong. He realized after thinking that it was an easy problem. He felt embarrassed for complaining about it. Oreum answered in a quiet voice,

(48) "☐ cm."

"If you wish, I'll go back to the tree log problems," Eunbi said as she watched Oreum withdraw in embarrassment.

Oreum still regretted blurting out without thinking. He felt bad, thinking that he had exposed a weakness to Eunbi.

"There is one 75 cm long tree log. How many 10 cm logs can you make?"

(49) "☐ logs."

"There is one 75 cm long tree log. If you want to cut it into identical 10 cm long pieces, how much will you have to cut off in cm?"

(50) "☐ cm."

"There is one 75 cm long tree log. If you cut it into identical 7 cm long pieces, how much is left over in cm?"

(51) "☐ cm."

"There is one very long tree log. If you cut it into 7 pieces, each being 1 m long, 30 cm of the log will be left over. How long is the initial tree log?"

"Hmm… I don't remember how many centimeters 1 meter converts to."

Seeing Oreum, she scolded, "You'll have to memorize this from now on." "I know. I just don't remember because you asked out of the blue…"

As soon as Oreum finished his sentence, he raised his hand and shouted, "Oh, I know now!

(52) ☐ cm."

Eunbi smiled. "Awesome! Math is starting to get more fun once you start solving, right?" she asked.

With a proud feeling, Oreum responded, "I'm still not too sure. But I think I can solve them now. From now on, I'm going to continue solving instead of avoiding them."

Eunbi felt that Oreum was gradually gaining confidence and was happy to have hope that she could turn back into a person.

I Was Almost Late for the Math Club

Compared to last week, the clubmates were playing around loudly, as if they had gotten used to each other. Oreum looked around the classroom once and sat at the same seat as last week. The vice president was already at his seat, seemingly working on something.

Oreum hesitated for a moment before gathering up courage and greeting him.

"Hi…"

The vice president looked at Oreum briefly and then looked back at his schoolwork. Oreum didn't feel as bad since the vice president usually didn't care for anyone else.

The vice president also walked alone like Oreum. However, unlike Oreum, he always seemed busy. Oreum wanted to ask him what he is always busy with. He also wanted to tell him to look up at the sky once in a while to take a breather.

On his way to the math club, Oreum stared at the cloud in the sky and was almost late for the club. After class, Oreum stopped to sit at a wooden bench under the wisteria due to the nice weather as he looked up at the sky.

The weather was warm and the sky was clear. It was so clear that it looked like an ocean. Oreum dreamed of himself swimming in the sky. Then, an airplane glided along the sky. Oreum woke up from his dream and recollected his thoughts. He thought immediately, 'Oh, that's right, the math club!' He grabbed his backpack and rushed to the club classroom.

The door opened and the sixth-grader from last week came in. As soon as he did, the chatting clubmates stopped what they were doing to look at him.

It was strange that they stopped to look at the sixth-grader when they didn't do the same with their teacher. The sixth-grader didn't say anything and wrote on the blackboard. The clubmates murmured among each other as if they had been competing on reading the problem first.

Oreum read the problem on the board. Oreum now understood why the clubmates were chatting silently. Here and there, they kept asking each other, "Why is he giving out this problem?" Some students faced each other, one student spread his fingers while the other student also counted his fingers as in the problem.

Even kindergarteners know that there are ten fingers. However, they didn't understand why the teacher gave them this kind of problem.

Now, the clubmates started chatting away. "Hey, you're a finger monster! A monster with 11 fingers~" some said as they joked around.

  Oreum thought of the teacher's intent behind the problem.

There are Eleven Fingers(?)

  You place both your hands forward. There are 5 fingers on the left hand. You count your fingers on your right hand from 10. You count 10, 9, 8, 7, 6. If you add 5 from your left hand with 6 from your right hand, you get 5+6=11 fingers. There are definitely 10 fingers, so what happened?

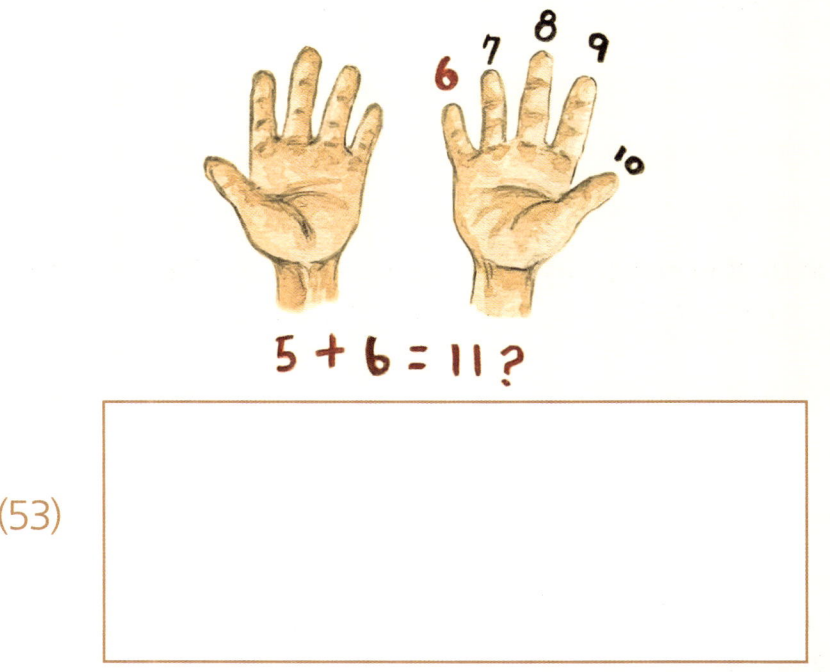

(53)

Teacher Jo's Talk Talk It's Multiple Questions

The following problems will be a bit harder compared to the above problems, but do your best to solve them.

These problems apply to fourth graders, but even the lower-grade students can solve if they have followed the book until this checkpoint.

You cut a 568 cm long tape into 70 cm pieces. How long is the remainder in cm?

(54) ☐ cm

This following question is for students in 5th grade and up.

You divided a number by 10 and got the remainder of 4. Find the original number that is greater than 50 and less than 60.

(55) ☐

Wow! You solved it even though you're in 3rd-4th grade? Excellent job. Can you solve this next problem?

When you divide this number by 15 or 20, you get a remainder of 4. Find the original number that fits in the range between 50 and 100.

(56) ☐

You were able to solve it despite it being hard? Keep up the good work!

Special — What Would It Look Like If You Draw Like this?

Tie the thread to the thumbtack and press down as shown in the following picture. Next, tie a pencil to the other end and draw while the thread is tight. What will be the resulting shape?

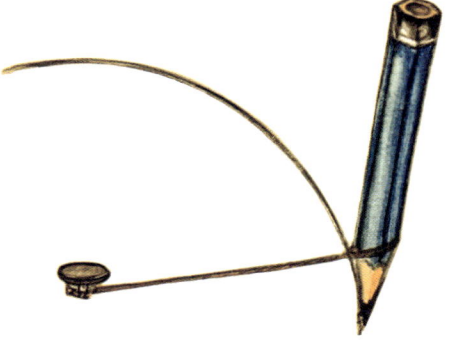

(57) Answer :

Tree Logs of Different Sizes

Oreum slowly walked down the staircase of the warehouse.

He hoped that Eunbi was doing well, also worrying that she would go through another muscle spasm. Meanwhile, Eunbi already knew that Oreum was coming downstairs.

"Why are you going down the stairs slowly? I've been waiting so long for you. Did you perhaps not wish to come here?"

Surprised, Oreum claimed, "No, that's not it!! Wait, but how did you know that I was at the stairs?"

Eunbi said, "Did you forget? I'm a zombie, so I'm sensitive to sounds. I can hear your footsteps just around the back of the main building of the school."

Oreum thought he came down slowly in vain.

Eunbi then followed with curiosity, "You don't come here as early these days. Have you been busy with something these days?"

"Yeah. I wasn't planning to tell you, but my mom signed me up for an after-school math club, so I have no choice but to be late. I was late yesterday as well because of it."

"I see. I guess it can't be helped. Let's begin our session now," Eunbi said as she picked up two tree logs.

Oreum thought to himself, 'She brought tree logs again today' and grinned. He thought to himself that he could solve any problem as long as a tree log was involved.

> "There are two tree logs of different sizes. The bigger log is double the size of the smaller log. If the bigger log is 60 cm, how long is the smaller log in cm?"

(58) "☐ cm."

Oreum then asked, "Are we now at multiplication problems?" Oreum now feels confident with multiplication problems.

"It seemed that you can solve multiplication problems with ease,"

Eunbi said, feeling glad that Oreum was becoming more confident. Eunbi moved on to the next questions, feeling excited.

"There are two tree logs of different sizes. The bigger log is triple the size of the smaller log. If the bigger log is 60 cm, how long is the smaller log in cm?"

(59) "☐ cm."

"There are two tree logs of different sizes. The bigger log is quadruple the size of the smaller log. If the bigger log is 60 cm, how long is the smaller log in cm?"

(60) "☐ cm."

Oreum answered while slowly picking up the blackboard.

"It's okay. If you still have trouble calculating in your head, you can write your calculations on the board." Eunbi was just proud of Oreum for doing his best to solve the problem.

"There are two tree logs of different sizes. The bigger log is five times the size of the smaller log. If the bigger log is 60 cm, how long is the smaller log in cm?"

(61) "☐ cm."

"There are two tree logs of different sizes. The bigger log is six times the size of the smaller log. If the bigger log is 60 cm, how long is the smaller log in cm?"

(62) "☐ cm."

"There are two tree logs of different sizes. The bigger log is ten times the size of the smaller log. If the bigger log is 60 cm, how long is the smaller log in cm?"

(63) "☐ cm."

"There are two tree logs of different sizes. The bigger log is twelve times the size of the smaller log. If the bigger log is 60 cm, how long is the smaller log in cm?"

(64) "□ cm."

"Do you remember that 1 meter is 100 cm? We solved a problem using the conversion," Eunbi said. Oreum grumbled because he couldn't remember that 1m was 100cm, so he remembered something embarrassing.

"For this next problem, you'll either have to draw or picture a tree log in your mind. Will you be able to do it?" Eunbi asked, being slightly worried. Hearing her words, Oreum was half-nervous and half-willing to solve.

"Let's just dive into the question." Eunbi beamd at Oreum's determination and spoke clearly

"My father cut a 1m long tree log into 4 pieces. He gave one piece to me. I divided that log into 5 pieces. How long is this smallest divided piece in cm?"

Before Eunbi finished speaking, Oreum picked up the blackboard, identified the problem's crucial point and started calculating.

(65) "The answer is ☐ cm."

Oreum answered with ease.
"Now let's take this tree log and apply addition and subtraction!"
"Adding and subtracting is easy."
Oreum said with excitement.

"I connected two tree logs of different sizes which added up to 60cm. If the smaller log is 10 cm, how long is the bigger log in cm?"

(66) "☐ cm."

"I connected two tree logs of different sizes which added up to 60cm. If the smaller log is 20 cm, how long is the bigger log in cm?"

(67) "☐ cm."

"I connected two tree logs of different sizes which added up to 60cm. If the bigger log is 40 cm, how long is the smaller log in cm?"

(68) "☐ cm."

"I connected two tree logs of different sizes which added up to 60cm. If the bigger log is 50 cm, how long is the smaller log in cm?"

(69) "☐ cm."

"This time, we are going to practice using the sum and difference. There will be a lot of problems related to this, so let's continue to work harder!"

"If there will be a lot, I'll just have to do my best."

There are two logs of different lengths.

1) "If you connect Ⓐ and Ⓑ without overlapping, what is the total length in cm?"

(70) "☐ cm."

2) "If you align Ⓑ and cut that length off Ⓐ, then what is the remainder in cm?"

(71) "☐ cm."

"Understanding from here on is important. The sum of the two logs is the same as the sum of two smaller logs and the remaining piece, right?

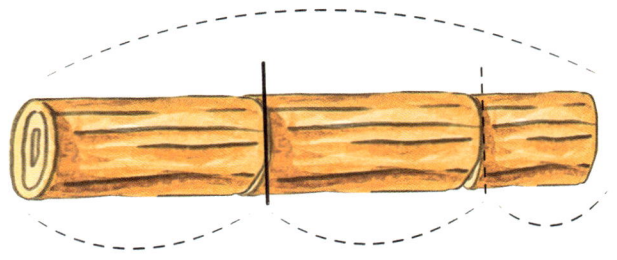

If you remember **(24+20=20+20+4)**, you can solve the following problems just fine. Let's practice that."

"I'm still a little confused, but I'll get used to it."

"Ooh, very positive-minded!"

"If you connect two logs of different sizes without overlapping, you get 60 cm. If the difference between the two logs is 10 cm, then how long is the smaller log in cm?"

"**Since the total length is 60 cm, the length of 2 smaller logs would be 50 cm. With that, the length of one smaller log is 50/2=25(cm). That means the length of the bigger log is 35 cm, which is 10 cm longer.** Since this is a hard problem, I'll help out with one more."

"There is a 90 cm long tree log. Two people divide the log among each other. One person receives a log that is 10 cm shorter than the other. What is the length of the smaller tree log in cm?"

"To solve this one, **subtract 10 from 90 and then divide that difference by 2. If you convert that to an equation, you get (90-10)/2=40, which means that the length of the smaller log is 40 cm**. Were you able to understand?"

"Yeah, I think so."

"Great! I'll leave the next one for you to solve alone."

"But I'll need enough time for this one. I might also need to draw it out."

"If you connect two logs of different sizes without overlapping, you get 120 cm. If the difference between the two logs is 20 cm, then how long is the smaller log in cm?"

(72) "☐ cm."

"If you connect two logs of different sizes without overlapping, you get 258 cm. If the difference between the two logs is 36 cm, then how long is the smaller log in cm?"

After thinking for a while, Oreum answered

(73) " ☐ cm."

"Do you understand now? By understanding this, the following questions will be easier to solve."

"The older sister and younger sister divided 12 candies among each other. If the older sister gets 2 more candies than the younger sister, how many candies does the younger sister get?"

(74) Oreum answered confidently, " ☐ candies."

"You open a math book, and the sum of the two pages is 177. Which page number is smaller between the two?"

(75) "Page ☐ , Wow! If you compare this to tree logs, you can say the sum of the two logs is 177 cm and the difference is 1 cm. It's amazing that I can solve a problem like this."

"So far, we practiced how to solve the shorter object, but there is a way to solve the bigger one. Of course, if you're still confused about getting the length of a short object, you have to practice more and get the length of a long object. Otherwise, things will get more confusing down the road."

"I just don't need to confuse myself," Oreum claimed with confidence, but Eunbi was still concerned for him.

"You know how to solve the short object. Find the length of the short object, and then add that difference here, and you get the length of the long object. So you don't have to be in a hurry." "If you add the difference to the sum, you get the length of two large objects. Following that, If you divide that number by two, you get the length of one large object."

"There is a 60 cm long log. Two people share the divided log, but one person decides to take the piece that is 10 cm longer. How long is the longer end of the log?"

(76) "☐ cm."

"There is a 90 cm long log. Two people share the divided log, but one person decides to take the piece that is 10 cm longer. How long is the longer end of the log?"

(77) "☐ cm."

"If you connect two logs of different sizes without overlapping, you get 100 cm. If the difference between the two logs is 20 cm, how long is the longer log?"

(78) "☐ cm."

"Since you got enough practice, I'll give you a set of problems with you solving only one solution among the short and long object. I hope you don't forget the solution to solving each."

> There are two sticks with a difference of 6 cm. If you connect them together without overlapping, you get 30 cm. Find the length of each stick.
>
> "How much longer is the longer stick than the shorter stick?"
>
> (79) "☐ cm."
>
> "How long is the longer stick?"
>
> (80) "☐ cm."
>
> "How long is the shorter stick?"
>
> (81) "☐ cm."
>
> "What is the length of two shorter sticks?"
>
> (82) "☐ cm."

"How much do you need to add to the length of two shorter sticks to get 30 cm?"

(83) "☐ cm."

There are two different sticks of different lengths. The longer stick is 6 cm longer than the shorter stick. The sum of the sticks is 10 cm.

"How long is the longer stick and the shorter stick?"

(84) "The longer stick is ☐ cm, and the shorter stick is ☐ cm."

"How many shorter sticks can you make with the longer stick?"

(85) "☐ sticks."

"Is it bearable?"

"It's getting easier to solve."

> Hyunsoo's 30 cm ruler is broken. Putting the two broken pieces together, Hyunsoo saw that one piece is 4 cm longer than the other.

"If one broken piece were 1 cm, how long would the other be?"

(86) "☐ cm."

"If one broken piece were 15 cm, how long would the other be?"

(87) "☐ cm."

"If one broken piece were 16 cm, how long would the other be?"

(88) "☐ cm."

"Find the length of both ends."

(89) "The longer end is ☐ cm, and the shorter end is ☐ cm."

"You're doing a good job! Then, we'll end today with one difficult problem." Oreum said as a joke, "I'm not doing anything too difficult."

> "There is a 260 cm long wire. You want to divide it into four pieces. Two pieces are the same length, one of the pieces is 23 cm longer than the two while another piece is 15 cm shorter. How long is each piece?"

"It's too difficult. I don't think I can solve it. Isn't it too sudden to give this kind of problem?"

"Right. It is indeed hard since you're finding lengths of 4 pieces. It'll be easier if you draw out the problem."

"It'll be difficult regardless, so just explain it to me!"

"Okay. But it's not hard as long as you understand it, so don't fret. It wouldn't be as confusing if the 4 pieces were the same in length. In other words, the wires of the same length aren't the problem, but rather the longer and shorter wires. One piece is 23 cm longer and another is 15 cm shorter than the reference piece, which means the sum of the different-sized pieces must be 8 cm longer than the two identical ones. If you understand up to this much, you'll be able to solve it.

After subtracting 8 from 260, divide by 4 to get the reference piece. It's written as (260-8)/4=63. The length of each identical piece is 63cm. Add 23 to 63 for the longer piece and subtract 15 from 63 for the shorter piece. The length of the longer piece is 86 cm and the length of the shorter piece is 48 cm. Lastly, if you add the lengths, you get 63+63+86+48=260."

"Ahh!! I understood it, but my head hurts."

"It's a good thing that your 'head hurts' from this. That means it's making you smarter."

"What did my head hurting have to do with getting smarter?"

"You feel physical pain when you exercise, but you gain muscles from it. It's the same with using your brain. If you just solve a little at a time to prevent yourself from getting overstressed, you'll get smarter."

"One of my classmates stops thinking when his 'head hurts.' So it's like saying, 'You can't get smarter. Stop thinking!'"

"Great. Let's solve another problem that stimulates your brain!"

"There are 2 logs that are 50 cm each and another 2 logs that are 30 cm each. If you can make different lengths by connecting the logs together, how many combinations can you come up with?"

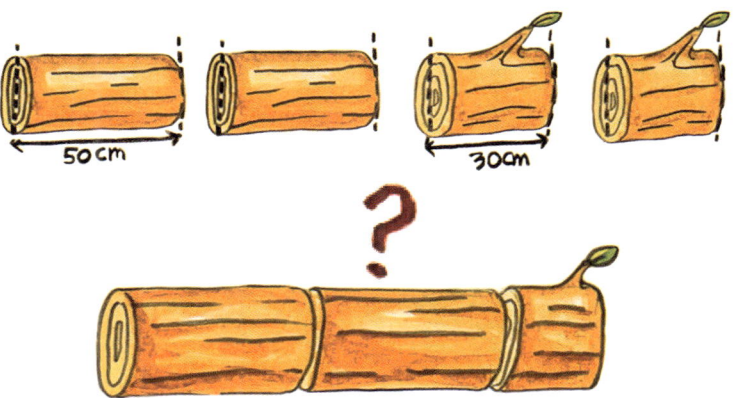

(90) "After thinking for a long time, Oreum answered, "I thought my head was going to explode. ☐ different ways."

"Wasn't it hard? There are cases when it's hard to understand when you see this kind of problem for the first time. Let's organize the work of the solution!"

First, the problem asked for the different lengths you can make by connecting them. So, you have to eliminate the scenario of using just one log.

Second, If you connect the logs, you can use 2, 3, or 4 logs at once.

Third, you count just the distinct number in length as one combination.

Fourth, it's easier if you start out with the larger sum of 4 logs.

- Connecting 2 logs : 50+50, 50+30, 30+30 (3 ways)
- Connecting 3 logs : 50+50+30, 50+30+30 (2 ways)
- Connecting 4 logs : 50+50+30+30 (1 way)

"You have to follow the order one by one and find each way like this."

The Rising Star of the Math Club

Oreum's footsteps felt light today. He feels as overwhelmed with excitement as one who is holding a huge secret to themselves. Oreum found the math club to be enjoyable. He felt confident after solving each problem and felt the desire to test his math skills again. He wanted to brag to the others that he trained hard with Eunbi. However, Oreum felt like no one would believe his story. It's just a secret between him and Eunbi. Instead, Oreum wanted to show his classmates that he can solve math problems now.

Unlike in the past, Oreum had the time to look around the classroom. Oreum observed his clubmates. His clubmates caught his eye in much more detail.

Among his classmates, the vice president was there, as well as the soccer kid, Minseok, and the president. Oreum didn't know why those people didn't catch his eye in the first place, but the classroom seemed small today. His shrunken shoulders felt wide open, and his face was full of smiles. Oreum wanted to talk to someone.

At that moment, the vice president hurriedly opened the classroom door. As soon as they sat down, they took out their practice book and pencil case from their backpack. Unlike usual, Oreum greeted the vice president with kindness, "Hi. My name is Oreum Cha." Despite Oreum greeting him, the vice president just took a peek before going back to his own work. Once again, Oreum didn't feel bad from the vice president's behavior. Oreum was in a forgiving mood today.

The sixth-grader opened the door and came in. All the students, including the president, who was memorizing English vocabulary, and Minseok who was gathering with his soccer friends and talking about soccer, looked up at the blackboard.

Even the other students whom Oreum didn't know well looked up at the blackboard. The sixth-grader just wrote a problem on the board without saying anything. It looked like a bunch of problems were written today.

The sixth-grader kept writing without stopping. After writing, he turned around and said, "It's not an exam, so talk amongst yourselves after solving. Help the ones that need help. I'll come back later and look over your work."

After saying his speech, the sixth-grader left the classroom.

The classroom grew quiet as the clubmates took their time to solve the problems. Oreum took out his practice book and started solving.

Oreum thought that his opportunity to show his true value had come.

Oreum felt like someone was staring at him. He looked up and saw Minseok standing next to him and staring at him.

Oreum asked in confusion, "What? Is there a problem?"

Minseok looked at Oreum in amazement and asked back, "You. Can you solve all of this?" Minseok thought that Oreum would use the time to doodle. However, he was surprised that Oreum was doing his best to solve the math problems.

Oreum wanted to say confidently, 'Yes, I can solve all of them,' but he answered bashfully instead, "I'm just trying to figure it out."

The vice president listened to the conversation and looked at Oreum's practice book. His eyes grew big and he asked, "Oh, that's all correct. You solved them perfectly! Did you really solve them by yourself?"

Oreum was surprised. It was the vice president''s first time speaking to him like this. It was more surprising than him solving the math problems. Minseok just looked in surprise at his two classmates. Minseok asked in astonishment, "Oreum, you solved all of this?"

Oreum couldn't say anything. On one hand, he was happy, but he didn't like people gathering around him like if he was a monkey in a zoo.

Oreum packed his things and left the classroom in a hurry.

Special — It Has An Interesting Shape

What shape would you get if you drew a circle with a string tied to two tacks like in the picture?

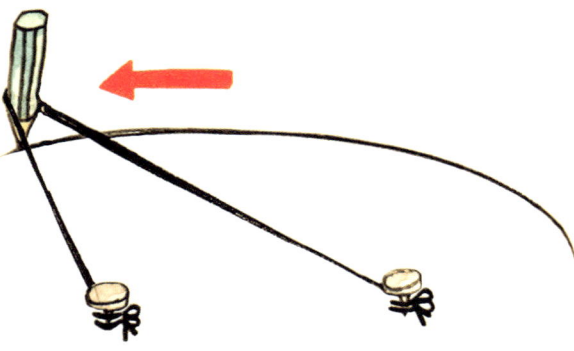

(91) Answer :

Teacher Jo's Talk Talk — There Are Identical Tree Logs

There are cases where you are told to solve **'identical tree log problems'** by drawing tables or making predictions. However, kids usually don't like to draw it out for themselves. In addition, if you tell your kids to predict and use a calculation
formula that might or not be correct, they will eventually avoid doing it. That's why I want to introduce an easier solution. It'll be easier for a kid to understand. Most of the problems in elementary mathematics are solved by drawing pictures like this and understanding the rules.

This is usually a question of comparing the price and number of coins and school supplies to the total price. When you understand, you can change the problems by **adding tree logs, use different sizes, and use simple multiplication and division**. After practicing several times, you can change the tree logs into coins or any other object. Stabilize the child's conceptual understanding, and expand the understanding from there.

Let's Change the Tree Log!

Although solving math with Eunbi became a daily routine, Oreum still didn't find math quite easy. There were times when he was confused with Eunbi's explanations. However, what was different from before was that he didn't want to give up after encountering a difficult problem. His head hurt at times, but he encouraged himself, 'Let's keep going!' at the thought of himself getting smarter.

This morning, Oreum's mom told him to come home after school and not run around too much outside. Oreum knew why his mom was worried. He didn't get along with his classmates and just walked around alone.

Oreum said to his mom as an attempt to make her worry less, "Mom, I'm always at the math club solving problems after school, so don't worry even if I'm a little late."

Oreum's mom couldn't believe everything he said, but she seemed relieved after seeing his expression. Oreum left the house thinking he needed something else to reassure his mother.

At class, Minseok approached Oreum. He looked at him with suspicion and said to him, "You seem different these days." After that, he went to his friends. No one else other than Minseok came to Oreum. Oreum stared at the window like any other day, and he constantly thought of running to Eunbi after school. He wondered what kind of math problems he would solve today.

As soon as the class was over, the children ran out to the school playground like a low tide. Oreum, who didn't like running, waited for his classmates to leave before slowly preparing to leave the classroom. Minseok and his friends seemed busy playing soccer today. Minseok was about to call Oreum, but he got distracted by his friend who tossed the soccer ball to him. After turning around again, he saw that Oreum disappeared.

"Where did he go? seemed suspicious…" Minseok said to himself as he looked around. No matter where he looked, he couldn't see Oreum anywhere. Minseok went back to play soccer.

Oreum, who was walking fast, slowed down as he reached the basement and went down slowly. Eunbi saw Oreum and was happy to see him. She was so happy that she grabbed the iron bars and shook them. With surprise, Oreum took a step back. Eunbi realized and stepped back from the iron bars.

"Sorry about that. I forgot for a moment that I'm a zombie. I was so happy to see you," Eunbi said quietly. Oreum said back, "You looked like you came closer because you wanted to bite me."

"I'll be careful next time," Eunbi said, feeling sorry.

Oreum, who had finally calmed down, talked with a concerned tone, "My mom got worried about me coming home late. Truthfully, I've been late everyday since I met you."

"Does that mean we won't be able to meet anymore?" Eunbi asked worriedly. "It's not that. So I told my mom that I was late all the time because of the math club."

"But my mom won't believe it wholeheartedly. What do we do?"

Eunbi looked at Oreum and said, "Let's think together." Eunbi thought for a while before saying, "How about you show your mom the questions we solved?"

Shaking his head, Oreum replied, "My mom won't believe me." "Then how about you work on the problems with your mom? You solve the problem and explain them to your mom." Oreum nodded in agreement.

"Okay. Hopefully my mom didn't worry anymore by doing this."

Thinking about his mom, Oreum was worried about how long Eunbi's mom and family would be waiting for her. "Isn't your family concerned for you? Wouldn't your mom be worried?" Eunbi said undisturbed, "Our parents assume that I can't contact them because of the research project with my science teacher. They also don't know that I am like this." Oreum heared this and thought that it was for the best for now.

Eunbi said, "That's why you need to be good at math. Let's start now."

As soon as she finished talking, she took out a blackboard.

Eunbi started to draw a tree log on the board.

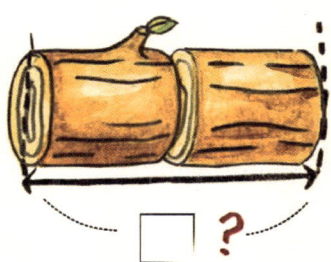

"There are several tree logs that are 30 cm long. If you take 2 of those logs and connect them like in the picture, how long would the logs be in total?"

(92) "It would be ☐ cm."

Oreum was curious about what kind of problems Eunbi would give out today.

"There are several tree logs that are 30 cm long. If you take 3 of those logs and connect them like in the picture, how long would the logs be in total?"

(93) "☐ cm."

"There are several tree logs that are 30 cm long. If you take 4 of those logs and connect them like in the picture, how long would the logs be in total?"

(94) "☐ cm."

"There are several tree logs that are 30 cm long. If you take 5 of those logs and connect them like in the picture, how long would the logs be in total?"

(95) "☐ cm."

"It's too easy, right?" Eunbi asked, giggling.

Nodding, Oreum responded, "I found the rule too. It's like playing a game with you." "You're getting good at this," Eunbi said as she continued.

"There are several tree logs that are 30 cm long. If you take 10 of those logs and connect them without overlapping, how long would the logs be in total?"

(96) "☐ cm."

"There are several tree logs that are 30 cm long. If you take 20 of those logs and connect them without overlapping, how long would the logs be in total?"

(97) " ⬚ cm."

"Aren't these too easy? I know my multiplication tables, you know,"

Oreum said. He wanted to solve more difficult questions.

"Okay. This time, let's solve a problem with는 **several 30 cm and 50 cm logs** in mind." Even though Oreum urged her to give harder problems, Eunbi was feeling happy rather than annoyed.

"There are ten 30 cm logs connected together. One log got replaced with a 50 cm log. What is the new total length of the ten logs?"

(98) " ⬚ cm."

"And what's the reason for the total length getting longer?"

"Well, if you replace a 30 cm log with a 50 cm log, the total length will obviously get 20 cm longer."

"There are ten 30 cm logs connected together. Two logs got replaced with 50 cm logs. What is the new total length of the ten logs?"

(99) "☐ cm."

"There are ten 30 cm logs connected together. Three logs got replaced with 50 cm logs. What is the new total length of the ten logs?"

(100) "☐ cm."

"There are ten 30 cm logs connected together. Four logs got replaced with 50 cm logs. What is the new total length of the ten logs?"

(101) "☐ cm."

"There are ten 30 cm logs connected together. Five logs got replaced with 50 cm logs. What is the new total length of the ten logs?"

(102) "☐ cm."

"There are ten 30 cm logs connected together. Six logs got replaced with 50 cm logs. What is the new total length of the ten logs?"

(103) "☐ cm."

"Did you find the rule? Fill in the blanks of the table and check that the length changes by 20 cm each time you replace a 30 cm tree log."

(104)

Number of 30cm logs	10	9	8	7	6	5	4	3	2	1	0
Number of 50cm logs	0	1	2	3	4	5	6	7	8	9	10
Total length	300	320	340	360	380	400	420	☐	☐	☐	☐

The following problem involves twelve 30 cm logs connected together.

"There are twelve 30 cm logs connected together. To get a total length of 380 cm, how many logs would you need to replace with 50 cm logs?"

(105) "☐ logs."

"Can you explain to me why you got that answer?"

"If you connect twelve 30 cm logs, you get 360 cm. If the length increases by 20 cm each time you replace one log, you will only need to replace 1."

"Good."

"There are twelve 30 cm logs connected together. To get a total length of 400 cm, how many logs would you need to replace with 50 cm logs?"

(106) "☐ logs."

"There are twelve 30 cm logs connected together. To get a total length of 420 cm, how many logs would you need to replace with 50 cm logs?"

(107) "☐ logs."

"There are twelve 30 cm logs connected together. To get a total length of 440 cm, how many logs would you need to replace with 50 cm logs?"

(108) "☐ logs."

"There are twelve 30 cm logs connected together. To get a total length of 460 cm, how many logs would you need to replace with 50 cm logs?"

(109) "☐ logs."

"There are twelve 30 cm logs connected together. To get a total length of 480 cm, how many logs would you need to replace with 50 cm logs?"

(110) "☐ logs."

"There are twelve 30 cm logs connected together. To get a total length of 500 cm, how many logs would you need to replace with 50 cm logs?"

(111) "☐ logs."

"This time, let's draw ten 40 cm connected logs and replace longer logs with shorter logs."

"There are ten 40 cm logs connected together without overlap. You replaced one log with a 30 cm log. What is the new total length?"

(112) "☐ cm."

"There are ten 40 cm logs connected together without overlap. You replaced two logs with 30 cm logs. What is the new total length?"

(113) "☐ cm."

"There are ten 40 cm logs connected together without overlap. You replaced three logs with 30 cm logs. What is the new total length?"

(114) "☐ cm."

"There are ten 40 cm logs connected together without overlap. You replaced four logs with 30 cm logs. What is the new total length?"

(115) "☐ cm."

"There are ten 40 cm logs connected together without overlap. You replaced five logs with 30 cm logs. What is the new total length?"

(116) "☐ cm."

"Everytime we replace a 40 cm log with a 30 cm log, the total length decreases by 10 cm. I'll switch up the numbers for the next one!"

"There are twelve 50 cm logs connected together without overlap. You replaced five logs with 38 cm logs. What is the new total length?"

(117) "☐ cm."

"Good job. Can you explain to me how you got the answer?"

"Connect twelve 50 cm logs to get 600 cm. Each time you replace a 50 cm log with a 38 cm log, the total length decreases by 12 cm. I'm replacing a log 5 times, so you subtract 12×5, which is 60 cm. So 600-60=540."

"Good job."

"There are ten 40 cm logs connected together without overlap. To get a total length of 310 cm, how many logs will you need to replace with 30 cm logs?"

(118) "☐ logs."

"Wow! You now mastered this. Let's solve the same problems this time with money."

"I'm used to logs, but still let me do it!"

Joohyuk has a total of 10 coins in 50won and 100won. The total amount of the ten coins is 800won.

"If all of the ten coins were 100won, what would the total amount be?"

(119) "☐ won."

"To get 800won from 1000won, how many 100won coins would you have to replace with 50won coins?"

(120) "☐ coins."

"How many 100won and 50won coins does Joohyuk have?"

(121) "☐ 100won coins and ☐ 50won coins."

"This problem is a variation of the problem of Hakgwisan ("Math problems using cranes and turtles" from ancient China) and will continue to appear from the 3rd to 6th grade of elementary school. So you should practice these often."

"Okay. I think I can solve a variation of these problems too."

Jihye pays 4000won and buys 23 items of erasers worth 200won and pencils worth 150won. Figure out how many erasers and pencils Jihye bought.

⟨Method 1⟩ Imagine all 23 items are erasers.

"If you bought 23 erasers worth 200won, how much would you have to pay?"

(122) "☐ won."

"If you switch an eraser with a pencil, how much will be reduced?"

(123) "☐ won."

"If you switch two eraser with two pencils, how much will be reduced?"

(124) "☐ won."

"To reduce 4600won to 4000won, how many erasers would you have to switch to pencils?"

(125) "☐ won."

"How many erasers did Jihye buy?"

(126) "☐ erasers."

"To confirm that you're correct, calculate (11×200)+(12×150)=4000(won)"

⟨Method 2⟩ Imagine all 23 items are pencils.

"If you bought 23 pencils worth 150won, how much would you have to pay?"

(127) "☐ won."

"If you switch a pencil with an eraser, how much will it increase?"

(128) "☐ won."

"If you switch two pencils with two erasers, how much will it increase?"

(129) "☐ won."

"To increase 3450won to 4000won, how many pencils would you have to switch to erasers?"

(130) "☐ pencils."

"Just imagine calculating (4000-3450)÷50"

"How many pencils did Jihye buy?"

(131) "☐ pencils."

⟨Method 3⟩ Draw a table and fill in conclusions.

Number of erasers	Total price of erasers	Number of pencils	Total price of pencils	Sum of prices
1	200	22	3300	3500
2	400	21	3150	3550
3	600	20	3000	3600
4	800	19	2850	3650
5	1000	18	2700	3700
6	1200	17	2550	3750
7	1400	16	2400	3800
8	1600	15	2250	3850
9	1800	14	2100	3900
10	2000	13	1950	3950
11	2200	12	1800	4000
12	2400	11	1650	4050
…	…	…	…	…

"Among the three methods, which seemed easier to use?"

"Definitely the first or the second…"

Special Did You Realize the Problems Are Identical to the Tree Log Problem?

Solve the next two problems.

Eunmi went to the stationery store and bought 500won notebooks and 300won notebooks. If the total number of notebooks are 12, how many 500won notebooks did she buy?

(132) "☐ notebooks."

Bokyung and Nari played rock-paper-scissors on the stairs. The winner goes up 3 steps and the loser goes down 2 steps. They started at the same place and played 20 rounds. Bokyung is 20 steps above Nari. How many times did Bokyung win? (Among the 20 times, none of them tied.)

(133) "☐ times."

Math Club: Still a Chill Vice President

As soon as Oreum opened the classroom door, the students all stared at him. Oreum turned around, thinking they were staring at someone behind him. There was no one there. The students were staring at him.

Oreum sat down quietly.

Minseok stopped talking with his friends to approach Oreum.

Minseok pestered "Hey, what academy do you attend? Tell me. I want to tell my mom and move there."

"I don't attend anywhere else," Oreum spoke truthfully, but Minseok didn't seem to believe him. Minseok continued to interrogate him.

"Then, is someone tutoring you?" Oreum didn't say anything. Oreum just knew that Minseok wouldn't believe anything he said. Oreum wanted to get up from his spot as soon as possible. Then, the vice president came in and sat down.

Minseok didn't leave and kept begging Oreum.

"Oi, Oreum! Just tell me. Share your secret with us and forget the times I teased you." The more Minseok talked, the more Oreum lost his chance to speak, and he found himself troubled. The vice president, who was observing the two, intervened and said, "Go to your seat."

Minseok was upset because he didn't get anything out of Oreum. "I'll definitely find out your secret," he murmured to himself and headed back to his seat.

Oreum was worried that Minseok would follow him and find out about the warehouse where Eunbi is.

Oreum then looked at the vice president who just assisted him. Oreum wanted to thank him, but the vice president seemed busy working on something.

Oreum took a quick glance at the vice president's practice book. It didn't look like anything that can be taught in an elementary school. The problems looked much more difficult.

It looked like the vice president didn't know that Oreum was looking. However, the vice president was conscious and looked up at Oreum and scolded him, "What are you looking at? Solve your own problems." He then looked back down at his practice book. Oreum was embarrassed for getting caught from peeking. He fixed posture and faced the front.

The club teacher opened the door and entered the classroom. The teacher stood at the front and said, "Did you solve the problems with the help of the sixth-graders?"

The clubmates answered, "Yes, teacher!"

The teacher smiled and said, "To clear our minds, shall we begin with a fun problem today?" The clubmates answered with excitement.

"I'll give a prize to the student who solves first."

The class is filled with noises at the teacher's words. All of the students were curious about the prize. Oreum was motivated as well.

"There are 10 stones making an equilateral triangle. Move only three stones to make an inverted triangle."

The clubmates started solving. Oreum began as well. It wasn't long before the vice president raised his hand.

After checking, the teacher gave the vice president the prize. The clubmates were disappointed, but Oreum thought it was fortunate that the prize went to the vice president.

The math club became more and more enjoyable for Oreum.

(134)

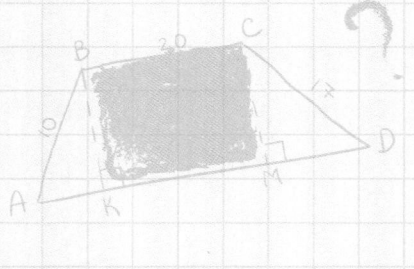

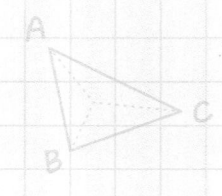

$2 \times 2 = 4$

Can You Fold It?

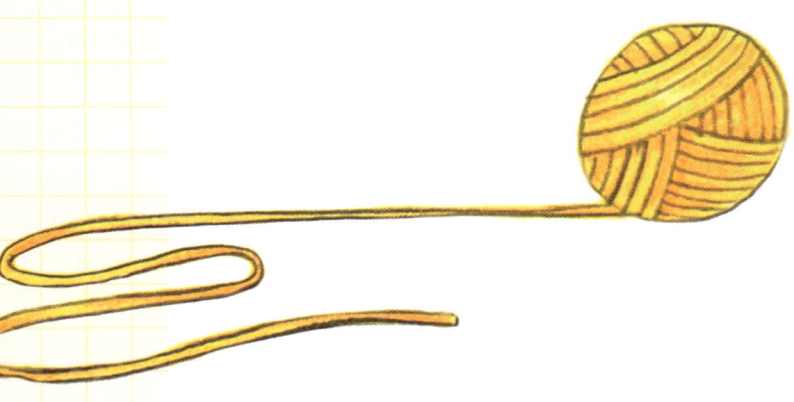

Teacher Jo's Talk Talk — Let's Cut the Thread

In Part 1, we used tree logs. **In Part 2, we will use threads.** When you cut a thread, you might think, **'What is the difference between cutting after folding the thread and cutting several logs at once?'** Even if you memorize these differences and solve them, you can solve them right away and it might be more comfortable. However, if you do so, you'll just recognize each as an independent problem and try to concentrate on the technique to memorize it. So if you focus on the commonality, i.e., the idea of 'how many times has it been cut?' rather than the difference between unbending logs and bending threads, it'll seem like similar questions

For example, if you bend the thread, cut, and unfold it again, it's like you cut a log twice. Of course, when you cut from a log, you remember, 'The number of pieces is one greater than the number of times cut.' No matter what tool you use, focus on **'the number of cuts.'** Threads, colored tapes, and wires are easier to fold and cut over logs. I created a problem using wires and threads to fold and make shapes.? If you remember everything you learned from Part 1, Part 2 will be easier to learn. If it's still difficult, go back and review everything in Part 1.

Focus on How Many Times the Thread is Cut

Oreum's mom held on to Oreum, who just woke up from oversleeping and told him, "Oreum, I bought you a workbook. I would like you to complete two pages no matter what your situation is. I won't be listening to your excuses," she said. "Yes, mom⋯" Oreum yawned in a trifling way.

Oreum's mom was surprised to hear Oreum answer so obediently. If it was like usual, he would usually come up with excuses or just go back to his room saying he was sleepy.

Oreum's mom brought the topic up again during breakfast in case Oreum changed his mind. "Oreum, 2 pages after breakfast, okay?" Oreum replied meekly again. "I said okay. But can I leave after I finish?" She responded with a smile, "Of course. As long as you return before dinnertime." Oreum plans to head to Eunbi urgently as soon as he completed his assigned workbook pages.

After Oreum's mom washed the dishes, she held the workbook and enterd Oreum's room.

She put down the book in front of Oreum and said, "Go ahead and complete 2 pages. I have the answer sheet with me, so don't even consider looking for one." Oreum began working on the workbook. The questions were nothing compared to Eunbi's. They would seem hard for him in the past because he never intended to think over them.

Meanwhile, Oreum's mom was checking him from outside. She was fascinated seeing Oreum so dedicated instead of dozing off or distracting himself with something else. Soon, Oreum finished completing the problems as he got up. Oreum's mom was worried that he was solving them half-heartedly and said to him, "Why don't you look thoroughly at the problems?" However, Oreum said back as he headed towards the bathroom, "Mom, I completed them so check the answered for me."

As Oreum's mom continued to grade his answered, she smiled. She was starting to believe Oreum's excuse of being late due to the math club. She wasn't as worried as before. Oreum noticed his mom's expressions and felt relieved that she wouldn't worry about him being late due to his sessions with Eunbi.

With light footsteps, Oreum headed to Eunbi. Despite it being a day off, the children were playing soccer today. Oreum searched to see if Minseok was in the group. Oreum was doing his best to avoid his gaze.

Thankfully, Minseok wasn't anywhere to be seen. With that, Oreum continued his way toward the warehouse.

Eunbi saw Oreum, surprised, and asked, "What happened? Isn't today a day off?" "I was curious if you were doing well." Oreum was too embarrassed to admit that he wanted to do math with Eunbi today. He also came because he was worried for her.

"What do you usually do during the weekends?" he asked. Eunbi said out of the blue, "Teacher Mole came here a while ago." Oreum got scared hearing this. If he came any earlier, he would've met his gaze with Teacher Mole.

"He knew that I was doing something." Oreum then asked in a surprised voice at Eunbi's seemingly worried words, "Does he know me?"

Eunbi talked carefully so that Oreum wouldn't worry. "No, he just knew that I was making a book about turning someone into a math genius.

He laughed at me, telling me not to just write a book and actually turn someone into a genius, and then he left." Eunbi seemed angry. "He locks me up after turning me into a zombie and then told me that in my situation.

That didn't make any sense!" She shouted. Her anger didn't seem to be relieved.

Oreum did his best to comfort her. "That's why I'm here." Eunbi realized that she was being too angry in front of Oreum and calmed down.

"I'm really glad you came here in the first place. Thank you, Oreum,"

Eunbi said with sincerity. Oreum immediately thought to himself that he should work harder.

Oreum always found school to be boring. No matter how much he thought about it, the thing that made going to school fun seemed to be math. Recently, he didn't fall asleep in class and it looked like the teacher stared at Oreum, more than usual. Including Minseok, other classmates also started approaching Oreum one-by-one.

Oreum believed that it all happened because of Eunbi. "My life seemed different after you taught me. I didn't only find math to be easier to solve, but I also found the attitude of my classmates towards me different as well. I feel like I can live my life now." Eunbi heard this and said, "In general, one problem connects to everything, so everything else gets resolved." Her words sounded like a life lesson given by an adult. Excited, Oreum told her his story about his mom.

"My mom was always worried about me coming home late. She then bought me a workbook and felt relieved after seeing me solve the problems."

"So how did you do?"

Oreum replied with pride, "What do you think happened?"

"So you did do well. That's a relief," Eunbi said with a sigh of relief.

Oreum was glad to see Eunbi being so happy. "So you don't need to worry about me leaving early. She'll assume that I'm late due to the math club," Oreum added. Oreum felt like he got closer with Eunbi.

"So what are we doing today?" Oreum asked. Eunbi's surroundings looked clean because the tree logs are all cleaned up. Instead, Eunbi was holding a ball of yarn. "What happened to the tree logs? Also, what are you going to do with that?" When Oreum asked, wondering, Eunbi smiled and said, "You graduated from logs. Now we're moving on to yarn problems." "Aww, the log problems were fun, though."

Eunbi takes the ball of yarn and bent a thread from it.

"If I cut the thread with the scissors like this, how many pieces will there be?"

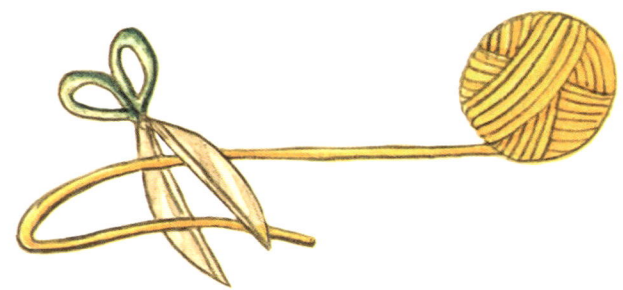

"Definitely 3." Oreum said, thinking that it's not any different from tree log problems.

"You weren't thinking four, were you?" Oreum heard this and denies. "What are you talking about!? I just said three." Eunbi said, "If I straighten the thread, you would think of it like cutting the log twice, so you can solve those problems easily. Let's start again."

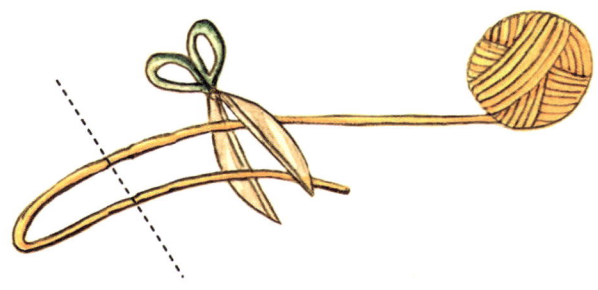

"If you cut the thread two times with the scissors like in the picture, how many pieces will there be?"

(135) "☐ pieces."

"If you cut the thread three times with the scissors like in the picture, how many pieces will there be?"

(136) "☐ pieces."

"If you cut the thread four times with the scissors like in the picture, how many pieces will there be?"

(137) " ☐ pieces."

"If you cut the thread five times with the scissors like in the picture, how many pieces will there be?"

(138) " ☐ pieces."

"If you cut the thread six times with the scissors like in the picture, how many pieces will there be?"

(139) " ☐ pieces."

"If you cut the thread seven times with the scissors like in the picture, how many pieces will there be?"

(140) " ☐ pieces."

"I found the rule," Oreum exclaimed. "It's a thread, but I thought of the rule I used with the tree log. So I was able to think of it easily." Eunbi said, "Yes, it'll be easier to understand if you remember the previous rule with the log. Remember that cutting the thread once is like cutting the log two times which makes three pieces?"

"Yeah. Also, cutting the thread two times is like cutting the log four times which makes five pieces." Oreum said, adding to the explanation.

"I'll try and write down the rule." Oreum made a table on the blackboard and filled each square.

"This time, I folded the thread two times for it to be cut at once like this."

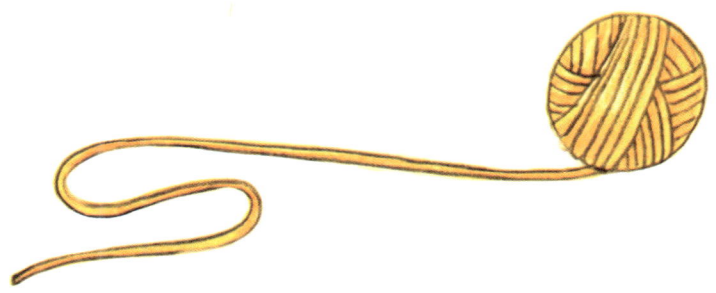

Eunbi folded the thread and showed the result to Oreum.

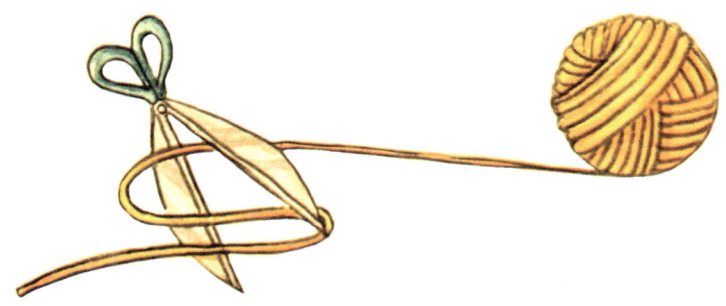

"If I cut the thread once with the scissors like in the picture, how many pieces will there be?"

Oreum stared carefully at the folded thread. Afterwords, he answered,

(142) "☐ pieces."

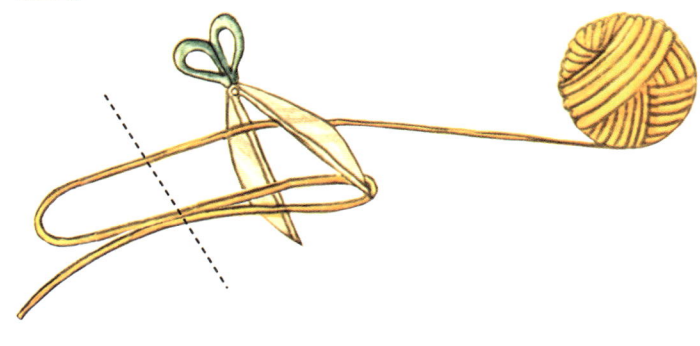

"If I cut the thread twice with the scissors like in the picture, how many pieces will there be?"

(143) "☐ pieces."

"If I cut the thread three times with the scissors like in the picture, how many pieces will there be?"

(144) "☐ pieces."

"If I cut the thread four times with the scissors like in the picture, how many pieces will there be?"

(145) "☐ pieces."

"If I cut the thread five times with the scissors like in the picture, how many pieces will there be?"

(146) "☐ pieces."

"If I cut the thread six times with the scissors like in the picture, how many pieces will there be?"

(147) "☐ pieces."

"Did you find the rule yet?" Eunbi asked Oreum without giving him a break. "Of course I did. And if I find the rules, isn't the rest just a multiplication table?" Oreum replied with ease. Oreum didn't tell Eunbi, but he had started using a calculation app. Since then, he had been

(148)

Number of times cut using scissors	1	2	3	4	5	6	7	8	9	10	...
Number of pieces of yarn cut	3	6	9	12	15	18	☐	☐	27	☐	...
Total number of pieces of yarn	4	7	10	13	16	19	22	25	☐	☐	...

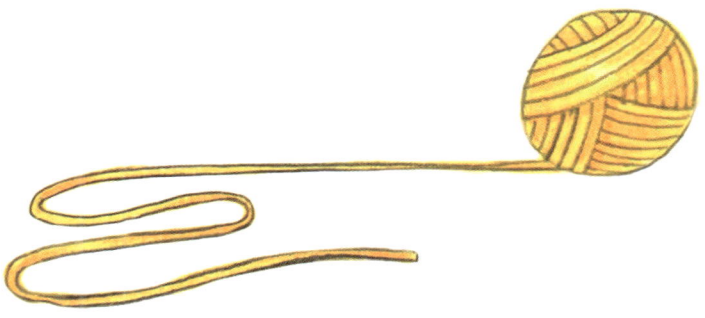

"If you understand this rule, the next problem may look complicated, but it could be easier. Now I'm really interested in solving problems with you." This time, Eunbi

folded the thread three times.

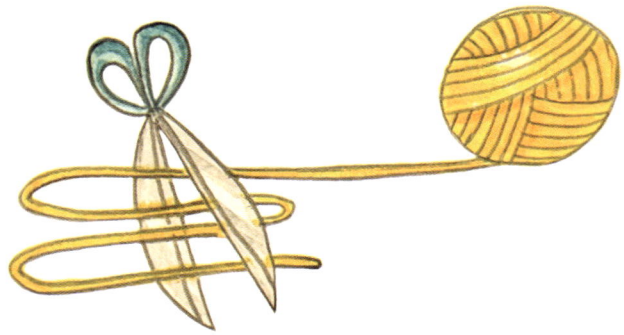

"If I cut the thread once with the scissors like in the picture, how many pieces will there be?"

(149) "☐ pieces."

"If I cut the thread twice with the scissors like in the picture, how many pieces will there be?"

(150) "☐ pieces."

"This is really fun. Looking at the drawings is also interesting,"

Oreum said with joy. As Oreum became interested, Eunbi gave out problems faster.

"If you cut the thread three times with the scissors like in the picture, how many pieces will there be?"

(151) "☐ pieces."

"If you cut the thread four times with the scissors like in the picture, how many pieces will there be?"

(152) "☐ pieces."

"If you cut the thread five times with the scissors like in the picture, how many pieces will there be?"

(153) "☐ pieces. I'm really enjoying this! The answer come naturally since I know the rule."

"Right? You seem like you don't need to draw a table anymore. It becomes easier if you focus on the number of times the thread is cut. The number of threads cut is the same as the rule in the multiplication table, and the total number of pieces made can be given by adding 1 to it. "If you memorize the rules of multiplication tables and add 1 to it without knowing the reason, it becomes a skill, but if you clarify your understanding of the rules, you will understand the principles. Can you tell the difference between skill and principles?" Eunbi asked. Oreum seemed to have vaguely realized the principle of the rules Eunbi taught. "I'm not completely sure, but I think it's a skill if you solve it according to the rules without knowing the reason, and if you solve it by knowing the reason, you solve it by principle. Was I right?" "Yes. Basically, solving without knowing the reason why isn't the proper way to study." Oreum became more confident knowing that he's solving the problems according to the principle.

Special — Wrap the Thread Around the Scissors and Cut

The following problems are of the same type, although they have changed their shape a little.

"If you cut the thread with the scissors, how many pieces will there be?"

(154) "☐ pieces."

"If you wrap the thread around the blade of the scissors once and then cut the thread, how many pieces will there be?"

(155) "☐ pieces."

"If you wrap the thread around the blade of the scissors twice and then cut the thread, how many pieces will there be?"

(156) "☐ pieces."

"If you wrap the thread around the blade of the scissors three times and then cut the thread, how many pieces will there be?"

(157) "☐ pieces."

Special: Wrap the Thread Around the Scissors and Cut

The following problems are of the same type, although they have changed their shape a little.

"If you wrap the thread around the blade of the scissors four times and then cut the thread, how many pieces will there be?"

(158) "☐ pieces."

"If you wrap the thread around the blade of the scissors five times and then cut the thread, how many pieces will there be?"

(159) "☐ pieces."

"Did you find the rule? Can you solve using a larger number? If you wrap the thread around the blade of the scissors one-hundred and seven times and then cut the thread, how many pieces will there be?"

(160) "☐ pieces."

Awaiting the Math Club

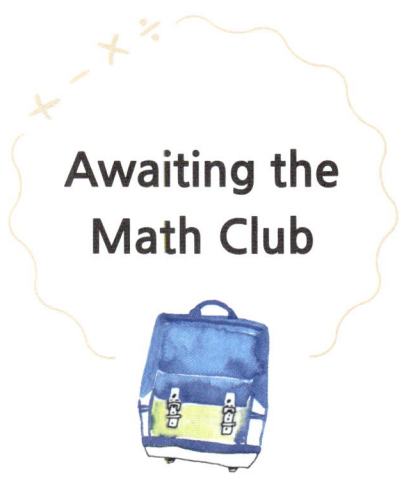

For a while, Oreum has been looking forward to the day when he goes to the math club. Oreum's mom asked him if there had been anything good going on when he was humming, but he just smiled.

After the bell rang, Oreum headed to the math club classroom. Just then, someone wrapped their arm around him and said, "Hey, Oreum. Let's go together."

It was Minseok. Oreum was dragged by Minseok as they walked with his arm still around his shoulder.

Minseok talked without taking his arm off of Oreum's shoulder.

"What happened to you?" Minseok continued talking as if he didn't understand what Oreum did recently.

"As far as I know, you slept everyday in math class and didn't study properly." He kept going without giving Oreum a chance to speak.

"But has the math god answered your prayers or something? Hurry up and talk to me!" Minseok pestered, while questioning Oreum.

Oreum, who was being choked by Minseok's arm, said, "Wait, wait, let go of me first-"

Minseok realized and releases his arm. "Sorry, dude, I got carried away. You still haven't answered my question, though. Tell me, since I can't help being curious."

Oreum answered, "Yeah, I've been studying alone recently. My mom kept nagging me since I was bad at studying." Oreum decided to lie in order to avoid this situation.

Minseok tilted his head as if he didn't believe it. "You're really amazing. How did you accomplish this by studying alone?"

Minseok and Oreum walked in the classroom together and noticed the vice president already at his seat.

Oreum sat down and greeted, "Hi." The vice president said back without looking up, "Yeah, hi." Oreum thought he heard wrong at first. It was definitely the voice of the vice president. After his greeting, the vice president immediately goes back to solving problems. Oreum wanted to ask what kind of problems he was solving, but he didn't want to interrupt, so he just stood still.

The noisy classroom grew quiet for a moment. The teacher stood on the platform after walking in.

The teacher then handed a bunch of test papers to the student at the front and asked him to pass one down to every student. There were a lot of problems on the test papers.

"The problems I gave you are easy to solve. They shouldn't be too difficult. I hope you think carefully over each one."

While the other students were struggling, the vice president solved the problems without hesitation. Oreum was also working on the problems. He noticed that he was enjoying himself while solving each one.

Oreum thought back to Eunbi's words. 'Even though I'm not a math genius, and even though I don't know what it's like to enjoy math, isn't it vaguely like what I'm doing now?'

Before he knew it, the teacher was standing in front of Oreum. The teacher saw the vice president solve the problems and nodded with a smile. Then, the teacher's gaze stopped at Oreum's test paper. The teacher smiled admirably again.

Special: You Have to Solve with the Definition of Line Segment

There's a shepherd watching over a flock of sheep. He must take the sheep to the water nearby, water them, and take them to the barn. Among paths A, B, C, and D, which is the quickest path?

(161)

Teacher Jo's Talk Talk — Do You Know the Difference in Counting Numbers Starting at 0 and 1, Respectively?

Zero and one are important numbers in mathematics, but they can be confused inadvertently. This time, I prepared this so that we don't confuse it. There are two cases for starting numbers: 0 and 1. For example, in terms of a person's age, one method is to mark someone who is born as a one year old, like in Korea. Similarly, in the West, you are considered zero years old on the day of your birth, and after a year, you are considered one year old. Those are the two ways to count age. The first floor of buildings in Korea is known as the lobby (zero) floor in the West. You will have to respect different ideas and study the differences according to each idea.

It's easy to say that if you get it wrong while solving these problems, it's because you make a mistake, but in most cases, you confuse the starting points of 0 and 1. It's rarely used for a while after dealing with these things in elementary school. But this concept will be used later to determine the number of sequences in the sequence unit in high school. Of course, the students who learn from me will practice under the name **'Number Counting'** as in this book.

Teacher Mole Knows My Name

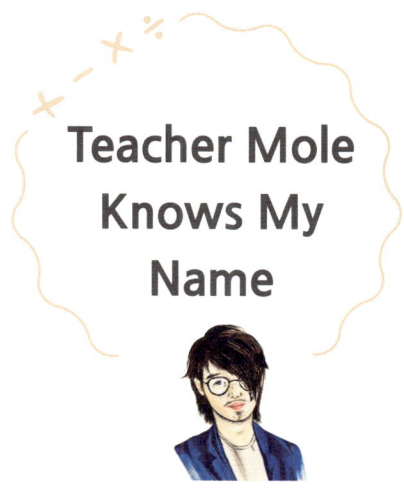

Today, there is a science class with experiments, so everyone is taking class in the science room. Oreum didn't feel like seeing Teacher Mole, but he had no choice. Usually, the homeroom teacher teaches science, but on the day of the experiment, Teacher Mole leads the classroom. Teacher Mole, who is always confined to a laboratory and does research every day, has been offered to come to many laboratories because of his special research achievements. For some reason, however, he doesn't leave the school to do so. He does not take charge as the homeroom teacher, but only researches in the laboratory, and teaches students only on days when there is an experiment. For that reason, the students call him "mole."

"There are rumors that Teacher Mole is working on something incredible," the students whisper. Oreum perks up his ears to check if the classmates knew about the basement zombie, but hearing the conversation, they don't seem to know. When the students arrived at the science lab, Teacher Mole was already prepared for the experiment and waiting for them. As soon as they sat down, Teacher Mole began his explanation for today's experiment.

"Today, we will conduct an experiment to distinguish between basic, neutral, and acidic," he explains as he held the glass tube with the solution on the desk. The students began to experiment in groups. Oreum's group mates were organizing the names of the colors on the paper that came out after pouring the solution. After staring at Oreum for a long time, Teacher Mole said, "The

experiment isn't even over yet, and your group has used up the indicators! Oreum Cha, come and take another indicator." Oreum froze in place. He thought, 'How did he know my name?' Minseok, who was beside Oreum, tapped him and said, "Oreum, he told you to take another indicator." Then Oreum came to his senses and grabbed an indicator.

Teacher Mole asked near the end of the experiment, "How did the color change when you added BTB solution to the aqueous sodium hydrogen carbonate solution?" The vice president answered, "It changed to blue." As expected, the vice president answered without giving any other students a chance.

Oreum continuously gave glances at Teacher Mole. Maybe it was because Oreum is conscious, but he felt like Teacher Mole was staring at him today, so he didn't even remember how he completed the experiment today.

After the experiment, Oreum immediately headed to the basement. He was scared of the thoughts of Teacher

Mole suspecting him. Oreum couldn't wait any further to tell Eunbi about it.

When Oreum hurried down to the basement, he saw Eunbi recording something.

"What were you doing?" Oreum asked. "Oh, hi. I was just recording how my symptoms have changed since the day I became a zombie," Eunbi responded.

"Oh, so you were writing a journal or something. Are the symptoms different each day?" Eunbi nodded, saying, "Although I can't tell the exact symptoms, they are definitely changing."

Oreum then followed, "I saw Teacher Mole during the experiment class today." Unfazed, Eunbi asked, "How did the experiment go?" Oreum said, "But, Teacher Mole seemed to know me." Oreum couldn't help thinking Teacher Mole's behavior during the experiment was different from usual. He wanted to tell Eunbi, but she said with a calm tone, "So what happened with Teacher Mole? Tell me more." Oreum replied, "Teacher Mole knew my name. He also keeps observing my group only." "What's wrong with that?" Eunbi asked. Oreum was irritated, thinking that he was the only one worrying about the situation. Eunbi observes Oreum's expression and said, "Teacher Mole is a genius. He can memorize your name after just one glance, you know? He probably knows the names of the other kids. So don't worry."

Oreum calmed his expression after hearing her words, but Teacher Mole wouldn't leave his thoughts.

Eunbi noticed Oreum worrying over Teacher Mole and decided to quickly distract him. "Oreum, do you think that numbers start from 0 or 1?"

Oreum answered, "Isn't it definitely 1? We always count from 1." Eunbi then said, "There are cases where you start from 1 and those where you count from 0. When we Koreans are born, we count from 1, but Americans start their age from 0 and become 1 year old after a year." Oreum nodded slowly. "So what are we doing exactly?" he asked with curiosity. Eunbi was relieved that Oreum's attention got diverted.

"I'm going to see if you can calculate well without

confusing starting from zero and starting from one." Oreum gathered his confidence hearing this. He still doesn't understand why the concept is important.

"Let's start with this question," Eunbi said as she shows a drawing.

"How many pieces is this divided into?" Oreum observes the drawing.

"9 pieces," Oreum answered.

"Did you just say what you said without counting the pieces?"

"No, I counted." Oreum believed that next time, he should get the amount without counting.

"How many pieces are in this drawing?"

"10 pieces," Oreum said confidently.

"Incorrect, Oreum. You said 10 because there's a 10 at the end, didn't you?"

"How is it different?"

"Look at the problem carefully. Watch if the count began from 0 or 1."

Oreum kept in mind the importance of the starting point.

Counting Numbers from One

"There is a wooden stick that is 20 cm long. How many numbers can you write if you draw lines at 4 cm intervals and start writing numbers from the beginning to the end, starting with (writing) 1?"

(162) "The answer is ☐ ."

"Isn't it easy to understand once you see the drawing?

    1   **2**   **3**   **4**   **5**   **6**

"Can you confirm that the end number is 1 more than the number of pieces?"

"Yeah, I can see it."

"I'll change the same type of problem a little bit for the next problem."

Eunbi continued to give out problems. Oreum found himself absorbed into this concept.

> "There is a 10 meter road. If each tree is planted in 5 meter intervals, how many trees are needed to cover the road?"

(163) "☐ forests."

> "There is a 20 meter road. If each tree is planted in 5 meter intervals, how many trees are needed to cover the road?"

(164) "☐ forests."

"There is a 30 meter road. If each tree is planted in 5 meter intervals, how many trees are needed to cover the road?"

(165) " ☐ forests."

"There is a 40 meter road. If each tree is planted in 5 meter intervals, how many trees are needed to cover the road?"

(166) " ☐ forests."

"There is a 50 meter road. If each tree is planted in 5 meter intervals, how many trees are needed to cover the road?"

(167) " ☐ forests."

"Did you understand? What if there are trees on both sides of the road, like in the following problem? Remember our usual problem with cutting 2 tree logs at once?"

"Of course I remember."

"Okay, let's continue."

"There is a 40 meter road. If the trees are planted in 5 meter intervals on each side, how many trees are needed to cover the road?"

(168) "☐ forests."

"Very good. This time, I'm going to flip the question around and ask for the length of the road."

"Okay. I'm feeling confident," Oreum said.

"On one side of the road, there are three trees planted in 5 meter intervals. Counting from the first to the last tree, how long is the road?"

(169) "☐ m."

"On one side of a road, there are five trees planted in 5 meter intervals. Counting from the first to the last tree, how long is the road?"

(170) "☐ m."

"One road side has seven trees planted in 5 meter intervals. Counting from the first to the last tree, how long is the road?"

(171) "☐ m."

"One road side has nine trees planted in 5 meter intervals. Counting from the first to the last tree, how long is the road?"

(172) "☐ m."

"One road side has eleven trees planted in 5 meter intervals. Counting from the first to the last tree, how long is the road?"

(173) "☐ m."

"One road side has thirteen trees planted in 5 meter intervals. Counting from the first to the last tree, how long is the road?"

(174) "You must think I'm solving the problems without reading them. ☐ m."

"Sorry. You were answering so quickly so I spoke as if there was a trap in the problem. It seemed you know the rule now. I'd like you to understand the problem, so I'll give out a few more.

"On one side of a 28m road, there will be a stake placed in 4 meter intervals. How many stakes should there be?"

(175) "It changed from trees to stakes. ☐ stakes."

"On one side of a road, there are twenty trees planted in 5 meter intervals. Counting from the first to the last forest, how long is the road?"

(176) "The heck, you changed back. ☐ m."

"You should now practice with larger numbers," Eunbi said. Oreum glances at her before exclaiming proudly, "Go ahead, bring it on!"

Although, In his head, he kept bracing himself while thinking, 'Oreum, get your act together! Just calm down and solve the problems.'

"One road side has thirty trees planted in 5 meter intervals. Counting from the first to the last forest, how long is the road?"

(177) "☐ m."

It took a little time, but Oreum was able to answer it.

Special — Solve by a Definition of Counting

The numbers are written in order on 12 stones in a row. How many stones are there counting from the 5th to the 12th stone?

(178) " ☐ stones."

Shall we move on to a problem with larger numbers? Did you say you don't want to? Go ahead and give it a try. It isn't too difficult.

How many natural numbers are there counting from 15 to 228?

(179) " ☐ natural numbers."

Counting from Zero

"Let's focus on problems starting from zero."

"Okay. I'll try to solve them carefully!"

"If one floor of a building is 3 meters high, how high is the building up to the 4th floor?"

(180) "☐ m."

You didn't confuse it with 9 as the answer, did you? Imagine a log standing vertically and start from the first end with 0. Isn't the number of floors similar to the number of pieces?

"There is a five-story building on the ground. It takes 3 seconds to go up a floor by elevator. How long does it take to reach the 5th floor?"

(181) "☐ seconds."

"Now, it's a matter of application, so be careful while solving."

"Yessir."

"There is an elevator on an eight-story building. It takes 6 seconds to go from the 1st to the 3rd floor. How long will it take to go from the 1st to the 8th floor?"

(182) "☐ seconds."

"Good job! I'll explain, so see if your thinking process is similar! To solve this problem, **you need to know the time to go up one floor. It takes 6 seconds to go from the 1st to the 3rd floor, so 6/3=2 (seconds) is the incorrect calculation. From the 1st to 3rd floors, if you think of it as a piece of a log, it's two pieces. So, the correct calculation is 6/2=3 (seconds). If we think similarly, there is a distance of 7 floors to reach the 8th floor.**"

"That's exactly what I thought."

"Okay. Don't get confused while reading the next problem."

"Cars with numbers 0 to 43 are in a race. How many cars are in the race?"

(183) "☐ cars."

"There is a car race across the desert. Due to the poor environment, many cars are disqualified from malfunctioning. 2 cars had a malfunction on the first day, 7 total on the second day, 18 total on the third day, and 30 total on the 4th day. How many in total are disqualified?"

(184) "☐ cars."

"You read the problem carefully! You wanted to say 57 cars, didn't you?"

"You must be a ghost, not a zombie."

"Eh?"

"It's nothing."

"Cars from numbers 0 to 43 race together. 2 cars had a malfunction on the first day, 7 total on the second day, 18 total on the third day, and 30 total on the 4th day. How many cars reached the finish line?"

(185) "☐ cars."

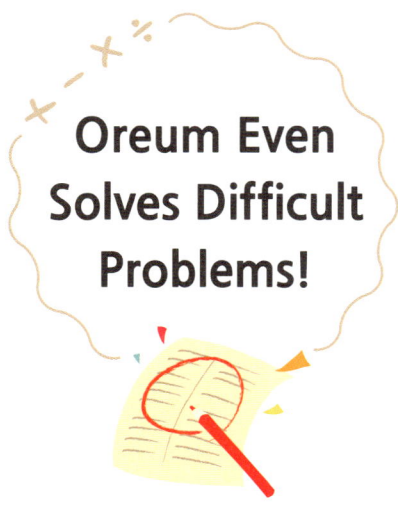

Oreum Even Solves Difficult Problems!

"You may have been able to solve the problems I am giving now, but the last one will be difficult. Still, I hope you do your best to solve it." The clubmates grew silent after hearing the teacher's words. On the other hand, Oreum was curious about the last problem. Time seemed to tick by slowly.

While the other clubmates seemed nervous, Oreum was as happy as someone waiting for their best friend.

Oreum was solving the problems at lightning speed. The last problem was difficult as the teacher said. Oreum, however, didn't think so as he read each sentence one-by-one. He even understood what the problem was asking for.

Oreum eventually solved up to the last problem. He looked up to see many clubmates still in progress in solving the problems.

He also saw Minseok sitting across from him. Minseok was seen scratching his head, frowning and agonizing.

Looking at Minseok, Oreum's smile spread around his mouth without realizing it

"Students, have you solved them all yet?" The clubmates answered like a chorus, "No."

"To those who did complete them, raise your hand, please." Oreum raised his hand.

Only Oreum and the vice president raised their hands. The students stared at Oreum in a strange way.

The teacher asked those that completed to step forward and solve one problem each and explain the solving process. Oreum went up and explained the last problem.

Oreum felt the gazes of his classmates slowly changing as he stepped up and explained.

Minseok was the most fascinated out of them all.

The teacher approaches Oreum and complimented him. "You must have studied hard. You did a great job solving all these problems and explaining them."

Oreum felt like he was on cloud nine. He never heard a compliment from a teacher before.

The others looked at Oreum with envy. Even the vice president looked at him.

Special — It's Not a Nonsense Problem

When people solve a problem and get it terribly wrong, they will say it is useless or a trap. In general, this happens due to a lack of concept or logic. The problem below is most likely due to an error caused by not being familiar with the amount of "multiple."

When you drop a drop of paint in a bucket of water, it spreads twice as wide every second. After ten seconds, the paint spreads across the entire surface. If you drop two drops of paint at once, how long will it take to reach the entire surface?

(186) ☐

Here is a more difficult question:

With the same rules applied above,

how long will it take to fill $\frac{1}{4}$ of the water bucket?

(187) ☐

| Teacher Jo's Talk Talk | # Fold the wire to Make the Shape |

Length and area are at the heart of questions to see if you know how to use terms such as point, line, face, side, angle, parallel etc. with shapes. This book didn't cover area, only length. However, you should strengthen your understanding of length so you don't confuse it with area.

You have to figure out the length of the perimeter of a figure, which may seem simple. Even finding the length of the perimeter of a rectangle burdens your child since he/she has to add four numbers (sides). Although, you shouldn't say to your child, "Add a width and a length and multiply it by two since a rectangle has two same widths and two same lengths." This is a formula which can be used to get a quick answer. At least in elementary school, it's better not to teach them shape formulas. Sometimes when the children are given a problem about the length of the perimeter of a rectangle, they try to have its answer by multiplying the width and the length. There are many parents and teachers who mistake this as their children not reading the problem or confusing the length and width of the perimeter. It's not because they mistook the perimeter and the area, but because they barely remember the formula that is taught and only memorize the multiplication. In order to prevent this, the children must have time to learn the shapes through breaking down and making/re-making them. This is a unit that is made to practice this, and I want to make sure that **"half the perimeter of a rectangle is equal to the sum of its length and width."**

Right now, we're going to use the length of the perimeter of the rectangle instead of the formula in the book, which is (length + width) × 2. Also, in the third year of middle school, the area of a rectangle is introduced as a quadratic function, and it's going to be used for such a problem like "when the area of a rectangle with a perimeter of 20 is called y and the length is called x".

Finally Learning Shapes

Oreum is no longer who he was in the past. He was confident in completing everything, and he didn't wander around. In fact, even if he wanted to roam around, he had no time because he headed to the warehouse basement immediately after classes. Oreum formed a habit of looking back at the school after stepping outside. He kept checking if someone was following him. Then, Oreum starts running as soon as he turned around. He becomes aware of his surroundings, as he wouldn't want anyone finding out about Eunbi. He even double-checks in front of the warehouse door if anyone is watching him. After seeing that no one else was there, he heads inside.

Oreum was always curious about what Eunbi would teach today and worried about whether he could solve it well.

He arrives at the basement and saw Eunbi still as a rock. "What's wrong? Are you thinking about eating me again?" Oreum now jokes with her instead of being scared. "Wait. I'm meditating… Saying that a cultured and successful elite like me wanting to bite people like a monster is just…" Eunbi sighed with distress. "Sorry, I was just joking…But how long do I have to wait?" Oreum asked, as if he was in a hurry. Eunbi then approached him.

"I just finished. I don't know how much longer I can wait." Eunbi seemed like she was holding herself from biting for so long. Eunbi took medicine from her pocket out of patience and swallowed the medicine.

"What are you eating?" Oreum asked with curiosity.

After swallowing, Eunbi calmed down after a muscle spasm. She then replied, "Teacher Mole gave this to me last night." Oreum started to get nervous after hearing Teacher Mole's name. "Teacher Mole come here every night these days. He brags about his accomplishments in the zombie project, even though I'm still like this." Oreum listened quietly. "Because I have spasms too often, he gave me the pills." Oreum was relieved to hear that. "But I have to eat one pill a day. He said that if I eat too much, the antidote won't take effect, so I'm doing my best to control myself."

"So I was thinking of eating only when you visited." Oreum wanted to comfort Eunbi in some way, but he couldn't think of anything to say, so he just changed topics.

"During math club today, the teacher gave out a difficult problem." As Oreum said that, Eunbi's gloomy expression soon disappeared. "What happened next?" she asked. "The clubmates were working hard, but it seemed like they couldn't solve them all," he answered like it was someone else's business. Wanting to hear more, she then asked, "What about you?" He widened his shoulders and said with dignity, "Only the vice president and I solved everything, so I went up in front of the class to explain it all."

Eunbi smiled hearing the news and said gleefully, "Of course. I was the one who taught you after all!"

Oreum stared in disbelief at Eunbi's self-praise. However, her words were the truth. If it had not been for her, none of the past events would've happened to Oreum. "Thanks. I was able to be good at math with your help," he said modestly. Eunbi answered, "No, no. It's because of your trust in me and your will to learn."

Oreum had the desire to solve problems immediately. Eunbi was pleased with Oreum's excitement as she showed him multiple steel wires, which were a triangle, a square, a pentagon, and a hexagon in shape.

"Today, we'll solve problems using these steel wires." Oreum was quietly listening to Eunbi.

"Here is a 60 cm wire formed into a large triangle. What is the perimeter of the triangle?"

(188) "☐ cm."

"Here is a 60 cm wire formed into a large square. What is the perimeter of the square?"

(189) "☐ cm."

"Here is a 60 cm wire formed into a large pentagon. What is the perimeter of the pentagon?"

(190) "☐ cm."

"Here is a 60 cm wire formed into a large hexagon. What is the perimeter of the hexagon?"

(191) "☐ cm."

"Did you find the rule?" Eunbi asked. Oreum nodded.

"Here is a 60 cm wire formed into a 120-sided polygon. What is the perimeter of the 120-sided polygon?"

(192) "☐ cm."

"Are you serious? Why do you keep asking these problems?" Oreum asked with frustration. "Calm down. I'm doing this because there are many cases where it's useful to ask the obvious questions. We'll focus on regular polygons (shapes with equal sides and angles), such as equilateral (or regular) triangles and squares (4-sided polygon with equal sides). Let's move on."

"There is a 60 cm wire formed into an equilateral triangle. How long is one side of the equilateral triangle?"

(193) "☐ cm."

"There is a 60 cm wire formed into a square. How long is one side of the square?"

(194) "☐ cm."

"There is a 60 cm wire formed into a regular pentagon. How long is one side of the regular pentagon?"

(195) "☐ cm."

"There is a 60 cm wire formed into a regular hexagon. How long is one side of the regular hexagon?"

(196) "☐ cm."

"You just need to know that you divide the perimeter of a regular polygon by the number of sides to get the length of one side. This time, I'll give out the length of one side of a regular polygon, and you give out the perimeter."

"There is an equilateral triangle with a side length of 10 cm. What is the total length of the perimeter?"

(197) "☐ cm."

"There is a square with a side length of 10 cm. What is the total length of the perimeter?"

(198) "☐ cm."

"There is a regular pentagon with a side length of 10 cm. What is the total length?"

(199) "☐ cm."

"There is a regular hexagon with a side length of 10 cm. What is the total length?"

(200) "☐ cm."

"There is a regular heptagon with a side length of 10 cm. What is the total length?"

(201) "☐ cm."

"Now I'll give out shapes with different lengths and widths."

"This is a drawing of a rectangle. You might have learned it as 'a four-sided shape with right angles (90 degrees).' However, the definition of a rectangle is "a quadrilateral with all of its four angles being the same". In order for all four angles to be the same, they, of course, are 90 degrees."

Oreum was listening attentively to Eunbi's explanation.

"How many sides of the rectangle contain the width?"

(202) "☐ sides."

"Are the two widths the same?"
"Yeah."

"How many sides of the rectangle contain the length?"

(203) "☐ sides."

"Are the two lengths the same?"
"Yeah."

"If the perimeter of the rectangle above is 22 cm, what is the total of width+width+length+length in cm?"

(204) "☐ cm."

"If the perimeter of the rectangle above is 22 cm, what is the total of width+length in cm"

(205) "☐ cm."

"Good! (Width)+(length) is half of the perimeter. It's easy but important information."

"This is nothing. Aren't you exaggerating?" Oreum couldn't understand Eunbi's emphasis on that fact.

"The most important things in math are easy, so it's easy to let your guard down. Students who learn how a concept or principle is used don't really know. It's a tragedy for those students. Only the teachers understand how important it is. This is why you should listen to your teachers. You'll understand eventually that way."

"There is a rectangle with a perimeter of 30 cm. What is the total of width+length in cm?"

(206) " ☐ cm."

"There is a rectangle with a perimeter of 40 cm. What is the total of width+length in cm?"

(207) " ☐ cm."

"There is a rectangle with a perimeter of 50 cm. What is the total of width+length in cm?"

(208) " ☐ cm."

"There is a rectangle with a perimeter of 60 cm. What is the total of width+length in cm?"

(209) " ☐ cm."

"There is a rectangle with a perimeter of 70 cm. What is the total of width+length in cm?"

(210) "☐ cm."

"You did good. Let's apply our understanding of length and width to solve harder problems, shall we?"

"There is a rectangle with a perimeter of 30 cm. If the width is 10 cm, what is the length in cm?"

(211) "☐ cm."

"There is a rectangle with a perimeter of 40 cm. If the width is 15 cm, what is the length in cm?"

(212) "☐ cm."

"There is a rectangle with a perimeter of 50 cm. If the width is 24 cm, what is the length in cm?"

(213) "☐ cm."

"There is a rectangle with a perimeter of 60 cm. If the width is 23 cm, what is the length in cm?"

(214) "☐ cm."

"There is a rectangle with the total width+length being 50 cm. What is the perimeter of the rectangle?"

(215) "☐ cm."

"There are several tree logs with three placed for each width and one placed for each length, creating a rectangle shape. How many tree logs are needed to make the rectangle?"

(216) "☐ tree logs."

"The perimeter of the rectangle-shaped flower bed is 48 meters. If the width is three times the length, what is the width in meters?"

Oreums's expression grew with concern. "I think I know, but it's hard." "It's because you didn't learn this yet. It may be easier if you were in sixth grade and you learned proportional distribution, but it's not impossible. Let's take one step at a time."

"What is the total of width+length?"

(217) "☐ m."

"Since I said the width is three times as long as the length, imagine comparing that with three tree logs for width and one log for length!"

(218) "It's easy now that I think about it like this. One tree log would be ☐ m long, so the length is ☐ m."

"Excellent job! While we're at it, let's try to solve sixth grade problems!"

"The ratio of width to length of the Korean Flag is 3:2. The perimeter of Yeongsu's Korean flag is 200 cm. Find out both the width and length in cm."

Oreum compares the ratio 3:2 to 3 tree logs by 2 tree logs. He found the answer after knowing that 10 tree logs are needed.

(219) "The width is ☐ cm, and the length is ☐ cm."

"Excellent job! You're my only student, but you're also my best one! Hehe. I'll give out one more. It's related to the area, but you're my best pupil, so I'll give it out!"

"There are 100 logs of the same thickness. If you use the shortest string that will allow you to tie around the logs, what shape will the string be?"

"Hmm… If I tie it, I might know."

"Correct."

"I was just saying it without thought."

"You'll know if you try it out, but when it ties to a circle, you can make the largest area with the shortest circumference."

Teaching Minseok

As soon as Oreum opened the classroom door, the other students looked in his direction. Oreum turned around to see if anyone was standing behind him. No one was there. They were looking at him.

At this point, Minseok approached Oreum, stopping talking with his friends.

"Oreum, just tell me already. How did you become this good at math?" he pestered.

Oreum was embarrassed, but he couldn't avoid him any longer, because he asked with sincerity. "Then, do you want to study with me after the math club? I can teach you the things I studied," Oreum offered. Although Minseok was glad, he answered, "But I usually play soccer after the math club…" Minseok still thought for a long time, and eventually answered, "Okay, I'll accept your offer. But you definitely have to tell me," as he happily headed back to his seat.

Minseok was in a serious conversation with his friends. It seemed like he was telling them that he couldn't play soccer today. Oreum saw the disappointed facial expressions in Minseok's friends.

Oreum took out his pencil case and practice book. The vice president said to Oreum, "Oreum, do you have your own secret to studying?" Oreum was surprised at the vice president speaking first, so he stuttered, "Um…. you see…."

The vice president said, "There probably isn't a secret. My academy teacher said that in math, we practice with a lot of problems of the same type. You did just the same, did you?" Oreum was still fascinated with the vice president. Coming to his senses, he replied, "No, I don't solve that many. But I do have that desire to, since math is now fun for me." The vice president handed out a paper and said, "Do you want to try solving this?" Oreum reads the problem written on the paper. He was no longer afraid of math.

After reading the problem, Oreum began solving it in his practice book. The vice president watched attentively at Oreum and soon said, "Hmm, you're correct. Why didn't I think of that?" he said, disappointed in himself. They talked about math with each other and grew closer.

"Are you taking any private lessons?" Oreum was embarrassed by his question. Oreum didn't study alone. He couldn't say anything about Eunbi, so he stayed quiet for a while. The vice president said to Oreum, "You don't have to answer if you don't want to," as he looked back down at the paper. Oreum felt slightly regretful, because it was a chance to become friends with the vice president.

Special — The Sheep Wants to be Free

In the image below, the sheep is tied to a pond.

This lamb wants to wander around the pond and eat grass. What is the minimum length that the tied string should be in meters?

(220) ☐

Teacher Jo's Talk Talk   **How Many Stakes Are There?**

Did you perhaps struggle while working in this book? Unfortunately, there will be harder problems incoming. The things you learned will be mixed together. For instance, there might be a problem with connected lengths and starting points included together.

Specifically, you might have to solve, 'How many trees do you need? You are about to plant trees in 4 meter intervals in an area of a square with a 20 m side."

By practicing this, you will develop the ability to use various variables according to the situation. If it's too hard, please review everything up to this checkpoint. You'll eventually understand through practice.

Support with a Stake So That It didn't Line Up

"What's wrong? What happened?" Oreum asked, worried seeing Eunbi crouching. Usually, Eunbi could hear Oreum coming down the staircase. She was crouching down at a corner, seemingly not feeling well. "What's wrong, Eunbi?" he asked again. Eunbi then slowly picked herself up and answered with a weak voice.

"Teacher Mole came by today. He said that my body is becoming more and more like a zombie. The muscle spasms are happening more frequently, and my body keeps bending everytime I walk. Teacher Mole said if I don't prove myself soon, I might live as a zombie forever," she sobbed with her face buried in her hands. Oreum was worried as well as frightened as he heard her raspy noises. He wanted to comfort her. "The semester is about to end. The finals aren't so far away. If I pass my exams, you can prove your statement, 'Anyone can be good at math if you teach the concepts and principles.' Can't you?"

Eunbi looked up at Oreum's words and went towards him.

"That's true. Time flew by quickly. Hopefully you'll do well on your finals. I'm in a hurry now. I'm in pain day after day," she cried, hugging herself as if she was in pain right now.

"I'm confident in passing the exam, so don't worry. You'll definitely turn back into a human," Oreum said, comforting her.

"Okay, I trust you. Thanks," she said with relief. She then changed topics.

"You said that Minseok from your club is studying with you. Is he following well?"

"Yeah, he's doing well. It's so interesting. He found math as fun as soccer," Oreum said with a grin.

Minseok would study with Oreum after the math club. Oreum would teach Minseok the way Eunbi taught him. Minseok found it boring at first, but he found it to be enjoyable after each day. He enjoyed it so much that he seemed to forget about soccer.

"Yesterday, Minseok was the first one to solve the problem! How did he become so good in an instant?" Oreum said. Eunbi followed with a smile, "Math can be taught by just teaching the concept and principle."

"And then there is the vice president in my class. I never saw him talk with anyone else, but he talked to me yesterday," Oreum said.

Eunbi then asked, "What's so interesting about that?" Oreum answered, "The vice president didn't want to befriend anyone. He usually studies alone. But he really spoke to me. He even wanted me to solve the problems he was working on."

Seeing Oreum talk enthusiastically about the vice president, Eunbi seemed jealous, asking, "So did you solve them?" Oreum didn't notice Eunbi's jealousy and answered.

"Of course I did. It was a problem he couldn't solve!" Eunbi was glad for Oreum, who was finally acknowledged by his classmates.

However, she was also feeling urgent. "You'll have to apply everything you learned, so don't feel too relieved." Oreum was always confident, but he always alerted himself.

"Three stakes are placed so that they aren't aligned. They're connected with a string. What shape will the string form?"

(221) "⬜"

"Four stakes are placed so that they aren't aligned. They're connected with a string. What shape will the string form?"

(222) "   "

"Five stakes are placed so that no more than three are aligned. They're connected with a string. What shape will the string form?"

(223) "   "

"Six stakes are placed so that no more than three are aligned. They're connected with a string. What shape will the string form?"

(224) "   "

"It's okay up to two stakes, but if three are aligned, you can't make that desired shape." "Now, give me an actual problem and not a practice problem," Oreum said with impatience.

"No, I'll give you two questions for review."

"There is a 50 cm string. A flower origami is tied every 5 cm. How many paper flowers can you tie?"

(225) "It's been a while since I solved these types of problems. ☐ paper flowers."

"There is a 50 cm necklace. A flower origami is tied every 5 cm. How many paper flowers can you tie?"

(226) "☐ paper flowers."

"Can you explain to me the difference between the two problems?" "With the first problem, the string is aligned, but for the second problem, the two ends are connected." "Very good. As long as you know the difference, you can solve those problems easily. Think carefully for the next one!"

"Twelve stones are placed at the same interval on an equilateral triangle. How many stones are on one side?" (There is a stone at each corner.)

"12/3=4, so 4 stones."
"I said not to answer so quickly. I'll explain in a drawing."

"If there are five stones on one side, the formula may seem like 5×3=15, but there is one stone at each corner. Each corner is overlapped, so subtract 3 to get 12." She continued with her explanation. "Let's understand it in a different way. Group 4 stones together using 12/3=4. Can you confirm that the number of stones on one side is 1 more than the grouped stones?"

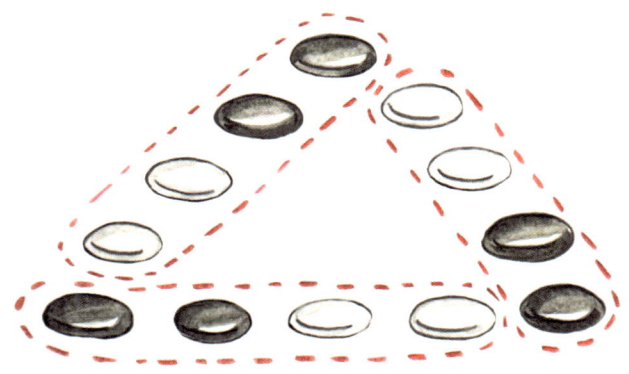

(227) "I understood. The answer to the problem is ☐ stones."

"Correct."

"But I'm not sure if that works in real life."

"That's why you need to practice."

"Twelve stones are placed at the same interval on a square. How many stones are on one side?" (There is a stone at each corner.)

(228) "☐ stones."

"Twelve stones are placed at the same interval as a regular hexagon. How many stones are on one side?" (There is a stone at each corner.)

(229) "☐ stones."

"If it's difficult, you can draw it out and divide the total by the number of sides and add one."

"Fifteen stones are placed at the same interval on the sides of an equilateral triangle. How many stones are on one side?" (There is a stone at each corner.)

(230) "☐ stones."

"Eighteen stones are placed at the same interval on the sides of an equilateral triangle. How many stones are on one side?" (There is a stone at each corner.)

(231) "☐ stones."

"Twenty-one stones are placed at the same interval on the sides of an equilateral triangle. How many stones are on one side?" **(There is a stone at each corner.)**

(232) " ☐ stones."

"Twenty-four stones are placed at the same interval on the sides of an equilateral triangle. How many stones are on one side?" **(There is a stone at each corner.)**

(233) " ☐ stones."

"Twenty-seven stones are placed at the same interval on the sides of an equilateral triangle. How many stones are on one side?" **(There is a stone at each corner.)**

(234) " ☐ stones."

"Thirty stones are placed at the same interval on the sides of an equilateral triangle. How many stones are on one side?" (There is a stone at each corner.)

(235) "☐ stones."

"Sixty stones are placed at the same interval to make an equilateral triangle. How many stones are on one side?" (There is a stone at each corner.)

(236) "☐ stones."

"You got them correct! We'll now practice with squares."

"Sixteen stones are placed at the same interval on the sides of a square. How many stones are on one side?" (There is a stone at each corner.)

(237) "☐ stones."

"Twenty stones are placed at the same interval on the sides of a square. How many stones are on one side?" (There is a stone at each corner.)

(238) "☐ stones."

"Twenty-four stones are placed at the same interval on the sides of a square. How many stones are on one side?" (There is a stone at each corner.)

(239) "☐ stones."

"Twenty-eight stones are placed at the same interval on the sides of a square. How many stones are on one side?" (There is a stone at each corner.)

(240) "☐ stones."

"Thirty-two stones are placed at the same interval on the sides of a square. How many stones are on one side?" **(There is a stone at each corner.)**

(241) "☐ stones."

"Fifty-six stones are placed at the same interval on the sides of a square. How many stones are on one side?" **(There is a stone at each corner.)**

(242) "☐ stones."

"This time, I'll change the words a bit."

"I'm about to place fencing around a square piece of land. If I place three fence posts at the same interval on one side, how many fence posts will I need?" **(There is a fence post at each corner.)**

(243) "☐ fence posts."

"I'm about to place fencing around a square piece of land. If I place four fence posts at the same interval on one side, how many fence posts will I need?" **(There is a fence post at each corner.)**

(244) " ☐ fence posts."

"I'm about to place fencing around a square piece of land. If I place five fence posts at the same interval on one side, how many fence posts will I need?" **(There is a fence post at each corner.)**

(245) " ☐ fence posts."

"I'm about to place fencing around a square piece of land. If I place six fence posts at the same interval on one side, how many fence posts will I need?" **(There is a fence post at each corner.)**

(246) " ☐ fence posts."

"I'm about to place fencing around a square piece of land. If I place seven fence posts at the same interval on one side, how many fence posts will I need?" **(There is a fence post at each corner.)**

(247) "☐ fence posts."

"I'm about to place fencing around a square piece of land. If I place eight fence posts at the same interval on one side, how many fence posts will I need?" **(There is a fence post at each corner.)**

(248) "☐ fence posts."

"I'm about to place fencing around a square piece of land. If I place nine fence posts at the same interval on one side, how many fence posts will I need?" **(There is a fence post at each corner.)**

(249) "☐ fence posts."

"I'm about to place fencing around a square piece of land. If I place ten fence posts at the same interval on one side, how many fence posts will I need?" **(There is a fence post at each corner.)**

(250) "☐ fence posts."

"I'm about to place fencing around a square piece of land. If I place eleven fence posts at the same interval on one side, how many fence posts will I need?" **(There is a fence post at each corner.)**

(251) "☐ fence posts."

"You already know that to find the total number, you subtract 1 (one) from the amount of one side and then multiply by the number of sides. To make sure you completely understand, I'll use a large amount of fence posts."

"I'm about to place fencing around a square piece of land. If I place twenty fence posts at the same interval on one side, how many fence posts will I need?" **(There is a fence post at each corner.)**

(252) After thinking a while, he answered,

" ☐ fence posts."

"Did you use the rule? Subtract 1 from 20 to get 19, then multiply by 4. Doing 19×4 may be a lot to do, so let's learn another method. If you group the stones like in the drawing, you can see that each corner is overlapped."

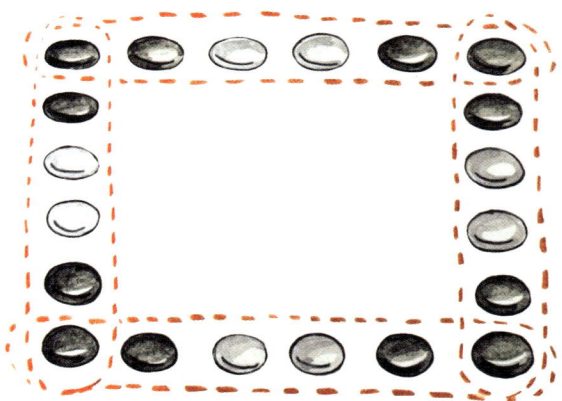

"Yeah, each side has two overlapped corners. Since it's a square, you get a total of 4 overlapped corners."

"So multiply the number of stones per side (6 times 4), and then subtract 4 to get 6×4-4=20 stones."

"Then if I use that method with the previous problem, I can calculate 20×4-4=76."

"Confirmation question incoming."

"O~kay~

"I'm about to place fencing around a square piece of land. If I place thirty fence posts at the same interval on one side, how many fence posts will I need?" (There is a fence post at each corner.)

(253) Oreum answered in an instant,

"☐ fence posts."

"Did you subtract the overlaps from 30×4?"

"Yeah. That's how I got the answer."

"You're right. To confirm if you completely understand, I'll give out two more."

"I'm about to place fencing around a piece of land in a regular pentagon. If I place thirty fence posts at the same interval on one side, how many fence posts will I need?" (There is a fence post at each corner.)

(254) "☐ fence posts."

"I'm about to place fencing around a piece of land in an equilateral triangle. If I place one hundred fence posts at the same interval on one side, how many fence posts will I need?" **(There is a fence post at each corner.)**

(255) "☐ fence posts."

"Good job! The next problem has several concepts mixed together."

You are about to plant trees in 4 meter intervals on the edges of a square piece of land with a side that is 20 meters long. How many trees will you need?" (Disregard the thickness of the trees.)

(256) "☐ trees."

"You learned different methods for solving. Did you ever confuse yourself about how to solve it?"

"You're right. For the last problem, I did 6×4-4. If you look at it in another way like using the concept of grouped logs, you can do 5×4."

"I'll solve it with another method. It's a square with a 20 m long side. If you imagine 0 as the starting point, you calculate 80/4=20 trees."

"There must be so many ways to solve it!"

"That's right. There are as many methods to solve a problem as there are a number of concepts. What seemed to be more than the number of concepts is just the addition of the number of skills to solve quickly."

"Now I understand what you mean by, 'Your math skills only increase by solving with a concept.'"

"Okay~! The purpose of solving various problems is to strengthen the concept. Instead of simply solving a lot of problems with skills, you identify the concept or principle.

I'm glad that you're understanding the ways of studying yourself! Let's solve more various problems!"

"You are about to plant trees in 2 meter intervals on the edges of a square piece of land with a side that is 10 meters long. How many trees will you need?" **(Disregard the thickness of the trees.)**

(257) "☐ trees."

"There is a 28 m road with a stake placed at a 4 m interval on one side. You are about to plant 3 apple trees between each stake of a road. How many apple trees will you need?"
(Disregard the thickness of the trees.)

(258) "After thinking for a while, he answered, "☐ apple trees."

"Since you didn't tell me the distance between the apple trees, it took me more time to think."

"That's right. Solving what the problem tells is the basics, and solving it with the taught concept is also part of the basics. It's not easy to maintain the basics. The core concept of the previous problem is 'counting from 1.' Since you're counting from 1, you get 8 stakes and it can be a seven-sided figure if it is folded. The apple trees are planted on the sides of that heptagon disregarding the intervals."

"I'm starting to get the hang of it. But I only understand when you explain it like that… I still have a long way to go!"

"It's hard to strengthen the understanding immediately after learning. You're doing really well right now, Oreum. But you must remember that solving the problem without knowing the concept is simply using skill. Got it?"

"Yeah, yeah, give me more problems, Ms. Eunbi."

"Sure, why not?"

"You are about to plant trees in 2 meter intervals on the edges of a rectangular piece of land with the width of 40 m and the length of 20 m. How many trees will you need?"

(Disregard the thickness of the trees, and remember that there is a tree on each corner.)

(259) "☐ trees."

"Did you confirm the perimeter as 120 m?"

"Yeah. How else would I have gotten the answer?"

"You're correct. I was just thinking back at your math skills in the past."

"You are about to place fence posts in 2 meter intervals on the edges of a rectangular fence with the width of 50 m and the length of 30 m. How many trees will you need?"

(Remember that there is a fence post on each corner.)

(260) "☐ fence posts."

Even Minseok Gets a Hundred

There isn't a clubmate from the math club that Oreum didn't know now. All the kids liked Oreum, and they always go to him for help. The biggest reason for this is because of Minseok. Due to him skipping soccer to study with Oreum, Minseok became good at math as well. The kids were curious about how Oreum taught Minseok. They ask Minseok for his secret because they want to be good at math too. However, Minseok just stays quiet, smiling. Minseok spends more time studying with Oreum than playing soccer. The kids no longer ask Minseok to join them to play soccer. Because of Minseok, who always ask to join him for math, Oreum has little time to take breaks.

In addition to Minseok, Oreum is closer to the vice president. It's because the vice president, who was once arrogant and cold, approaches Oreum. To him, Minseok and the vice president are both friends.

Today, the teacher asked the students, "Did you do well on your finals?" The classmates didn't say anything.

"I just graded the exams, and came to announce that three people aced the exam."

Everyone knew who those three students were without the teacher officially announcing.

"As you all thought, those three are the vice president, Oreum Cha, and Minseok Kim. Oreum and Minseok especially increased their grades significantly. I hope the rest of you can get good results like those two."

After class, Oreum, Minseok, and the vice president met the club teacher while passing through the hallway.

"I heard that Oreum and Minseok got a hundred. Is that true?"

"Teacher, the vice president also got a hundred. Also, how did you know that we aced the finals?"

"The vice president always gets a hundred. Your homeroom teacher kept complimenting Oreum's and Minseok's efforts, so all of the teachers know. And I would appreciate it if the three of you can run the club for the second semester. I'll only help when you three need assistance. How does that sound?" the teacher asked. Then, a few clubmates around them answered in unison, "Yes, we're okay with it." The clubmates, who wanted to know the concepts from Oreum, were happy to hear the teacher's suggestion.

The teacher stood beside Oreum and the vice president

and said, "I hope you can successfully lead the math club." They replied, "Yes, we'll do our best." They looked at each other and smiled.

Oreum wanted to share the good news with Eunbi. Eunbi could turn back into a human. He remembered Teacher Mole's promise to cure her.

Oreum thought of how to distract his friends to leave the club. However, Minseok urges him to celebrate together by eating rice cakes. Oreum had no choice but to lie, "My mom wants me to head home early, so let's eat tomorrow." Minseok didn't listen and continued to persuade him. With no other option, Oreum immediately notified Minseok and headed to the direction of his house without hearing Minseok's answer. After running for a while, as he couldn't see Minseok and the vice president, Oreum turned around and headed back to the school.

Oreum hurriedly headed down the staircase. He looked around with worry. However, there wasn't anyone there. Oreum collapsed on the spot.

"…What's going on? There must be a mistake… In the end, it was impossible to turn Eunbi back into a human!" Oreum cries, still sitting down.

He then thought, 'Or, was it my fault? Did I not work hard enough? How is Eunbi doing, anyway? Although she's still a zombie, shouldn't she be here?" Oreum was wondering to himself if he was dreaming the entire time. Then, he thought back to the mistakes he might have committed.

The basement was so clean that it looked like nothing had happened for the past few days. There were no traces of Eunbi. The iron bars that separated Oreum and Eunbi were gone, and there were no longer any scratches from Eunbi's muscle spasms on the wall. There was another difference. The basement that had always felt dark is now lit. It was easier to see the surrounding details. It was bright because of the sunlight coming from the window on the upper left corner.

Oreum stares blankly in the basement. He didn't know what to do. He also felt like it was not right to head home just yet. Overwhelmed with worries for Eunbi, he couldn't move an inch.

He had a bad feeling. Just then, someone was walking down the stairs. Someone was coming. Oreum looked around for a place to hide, but everything was removed, so he could only stay at his spot. He thought that Teacher Mole would be coming down here. Oreum was frightened, not knowing how to confront him. When he thought about what to do if Teacher Mole experimented with turning him into a zombie, he also remembers Eunbi twisting her body and screaming and suffering while having muscle spasms as a zombie, and Oreum's body began to tremble in fear.

However, the footsteps didn't sound like a singular person. Oreum saw two people standing across from him. It was Teacher Mole and a pretty girl. Oreum asked slowly, "Are you Eunbi?" "Yes, I am." Teacher Mole and Eunbi saw the surprised Oreum and laughed.

"Are you okay? Are you a person? Do you know how worried I was? How could you disappear on me without telling me!?" Mixture of relief and anger overwhelms Oreum. "Why would I disappear? I came here to let you know first."

"I thought something happened to you since you weren't there…"

Oreum's eyes were teary. Teacher Mole then said, "I may be cranky, but I'm not a bad person." Oreum forgot for a second that Teacher Mole was beside them. "No, I mean… Teacher, I'm sorry,"

Oreum said, embarrassed.

Eunbi spoke up next.

"First, calm down… I'll tell you everything." After Oreum calmed down, Eunbi began explaining. "Today, after the finals, the Teacher Mole immediately requested the homeroom teacher to grade Oreum's paper first. He even checked the progress of the math club through the math club teacher." After glancing at Teacher Mole, she looked back at Oreum and continued speaking. "Teacher Mole said that he immediately prepared the antidote before turning me into a zombie. He was going to cure me immediately after, but he saw you coming down the basement and used the opportunity to have me prove my own statement."

"Then he knew about me visiting you everyday?" Oreum asked, even more surprised than before.

"He also heard our conversations. He was curious about how I teach you math and your reaction to me as a zombie." Although Eunbi was calm, Oreum still couldn't

accept the entire situation.

He was just glad that Eunbi is no longer a zombie.

"Oreum Cha, you were amazing."

Teacher Mole complimented him.

"It's all thanks to Eunbi."

"Yes, now I'm convinced by Eunbi's words. So one can indeed do good in math if they understand the principle and concepts. I also learned through you: 'A genius is a slow-bloomed gifted child.'"

Oreum is now a student who is no longer afraid of math problems and solves them through concepts and principles. Eunbi taught him that solving math this way will make him better at math than anyone else. Teacher Mole praised that at this rate of development, Oreum might surpass Eunbi, the original math genius. Eunbi said with a big smile, "A disciple surpassing his own teacher is the best compliment to the teacher". It was a happy afternoon for Cha Oreum, a newborn math genius.

Special   It's a Nostalgic Matchstick Problem

This last question is a problem I (author) solved in high school. There are multiple answered, and some can be solved alone while others need the assistance of an adult. Solve this with your family!

The following arrangement of the matchsticks is a miscalculation. Use One more matchstick to make the equation correct. There are three answered. (The parents have two more answered to figure out, and this problem defines rounding in the third place after the decimal point as equal.)

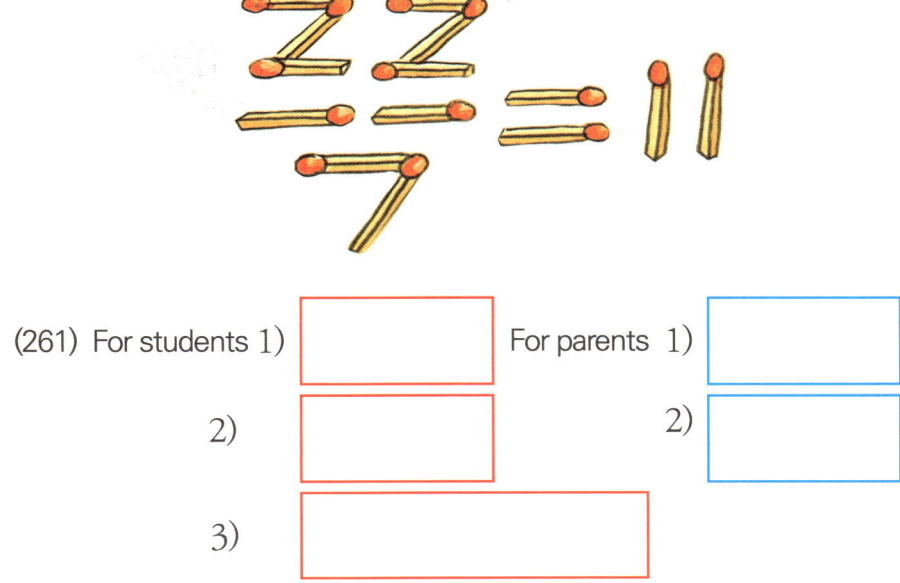

(261) For students 1) ☐   For parents 1) ☐

2) ☐   2) ☐

3) ☐

A Magical Fairytale for
All Elementary School Students

The Rise of a Math Genius

Answers

(1) 2 (2) 3 (3) 4 (4) 5 (5) 6 (6) 7 (7) 8 (8) 8, 9 (9) 101 (10) 791 (11) 1 (12) 2 (13) 3 (14) 4 (15) 5 (16) 6 (17) 7, 8 (18) 4 (19) 8 (20) 12 (21) 16 (22) 20 (23) 7, 4, 6 × 4, 7 × 4 (24) 49 (25) 47 (26) 4 (27) 6 (28) 8 (29) 10 (30) 12 (31) 8, 9, 14, 16, 18 (32) 6 (33) 9 (34) 12 (35) 15 (36) 18 (37) 8, 9, 21, 24, 27 (38) 24 (39) 7 (40) 16

(41) 3minutes before (A), before (B) / 3minutes after (A), before (C) / 3minutes after (B), after (C)

(42) 40 (43) 30 (44) 20 (45) 15 (46) 12 (47) 10 (48) 1 (49) 7 (50) 5 (51) 5 (52) 730

(53) If you count backwards, you get 6 on your fifth finger. It's just the counting order, not the number of fingers.

(54) 8 (55) 54 (56) 64

(57) If you count backwards, you get 6 on your fifth finger. It's just the counting order, not the number of fingers.

(58) 30 **(59)** 20 **(60)** 15 **(61)** 12 **(62)** 10 **(63)** 6 **(64)** 5 **(65)** 5 **(66)** 50 **(67)** 40 **(68)** 20 **(69)** 10 **(70)** 44 **(71)** 4 **(72)** 50 **(73)** 111 **(74)** 5 **(75)** 88 **(76)** 35 **(77)** 50 **(78)** 60 **(79)** 6 **(80)** 18 **(81)** 12 **(82)** 24 **(83)** 6 **(84)** 8, 2 **(85)** 4 **(86)** 29 **(87)** 15 **(88)** 14 **(89)** 17, 13 **(90)** 6

(91) Ellipse (Definition of an ellipse: a collection of points where the sum of its distances from two fixed points is constant; however, the sum of the distances is longer than the distance between the two points.) Students would have drawn a circle with threads or compasses. But I put it in here because I thought there would be no students who have drawn an ellipse. The shape of the ellipse can be said to have crushed the circle, and the name contains the word circle, but it's not a circle.

(92) 60 **(93)** 90 **(94)** 120 **(95)** 150 **(96)** 300 **(97)** 600 **(98)** 320 **(99)** 340 **(100)** 360 **(101)** 380 **(102)** 400 **(103)** 420 **(104)** 440, 460, 480, 500 **(105)** 1 **(106)** 2 **(107)**

3 **(108)** 4 **(109)** 5 **(110)** 6 **(111)** 7 **(112)** 390 **(113)** 380 **(114)** 370 **(115)** 360 **(116)** 350 **(117)** 540 **(118)** 9 **(119)** 1000 **(120)** 4 **(121)** 6, 4 **(122)** 4600 **(123)** 50 **(124)** 100 **(125)** 12 **(126)** 11 **(127)** 3450 **(128)** 50 **(129)** 100 **(130)** 11 **(131)** 12

(132) 7 (5000−3600)÷200 = 7

Don't confuse the 500 won count with the 300 won count. Was it too difficult? Did you feel that as the grade goes up, only the numbers change, but the same problems continue? So didn't you feel it was good to practice enough when the number was small?

(133) 12

If Bokyung won 20 times, she would go up 60 steps instead of 20. But losing results in going down five steps each. For 60 to be 20, there needs to be 40 less, and to decrease by 40, divide 40/5 = losing 8 times. That means 20−8 = winning 12 times. To confirm: (12×3)−(8×2) = 20.

(134)

(135) 5 (136) 7 (137) 9 (138) 11 (139) 13 (140) 15 (141) 14, 16, 20, 19, 21 (142) 4 (143) 7 (144) 10 (145) 13 (146) 16 (147) 19 (148) 21, 24, 30, 28, 31 (149) 5 (150) 9 (151) 13 (152) 17 (153) 21 (154) 2 (155) 3 (156) 4 (157) 5 (158) 6 (159) 7 (160) 109

(161)

axis of symmetry

(A) (B) (C) (D)

C (Definition of line segment : the line that draws closest between two different points; therefore, the longest side of a triangle is always shorter than the sum of the lengths of the other two sides.) Connecting two fixed points P, Q and one of points A, B, C and D makes a different triangle each time, but all triangles made are isosceles triangles. Also, the longest side of a triangle is always shorter than the sum of the lengths of the other two sides. Therefore, C is the fastest path.

(162) 6 (163) 3 (164) 5 (165) 7 (166) 9 (167) 11 (168) 18

(169) 10 **(170)** 20 **(171)** 30 **(172)** 40 **(173)** 50 **(174)** 50 **(175)** 8 **(176)** 45 **(177)** 145 **(178)** 8

Did you perhaps think of subtracting 5 from 12 to get 7? You can get the right answer by counting, but it can be solved by applying the principle. Here is the solution. Counting from 1 to 12 results in 12 numbers. One less than 5 is 4. Since you start counting from 5, you subtract 4 to get 8. If you would like to try, apply Anho Jo's idea, '1,2,3⋯ the last number is the total amount.' You can learn more on Anho Jo's Youtube channel.

(179) 214

If you solve it by definition, you have to start with 1, 2, 3, so you can see the answer by subtracting 14 from each number.

(180) 12 **(181)** 12 **(182)** 21 **(183)** 44 **(184)** 30 **(185)** 14 **(186)** 9 seconds

Did you perhaps think that it is 5 seconds because it is half of 10? If you drop one, it becomes twice the width in a second, so the answer is 9.

(187) 8 seconds (188) 60 (189) 60 (190) 60 (191) 60 (192) 60 (193) 20 (194) 15 (195) 12 (196) 10 (197) 30 (198) 40 (199) 50 (200) 60 (201) 70 (202) 2 (203) 2 (204) 22 (205) 11 (206) 15 (207) 20 (208) 25 (209) 30 (210) 35 (211) 5 (212) 5 (213) 1 (214) 7 (215) 100 (216) 8 (217) 24 (218) 6, 18 (219) 60, 40 (220) 13m

A stake is lodged somewhere by the pond. Even so, with a 13m leash, which is half the length of the entire perimeter, you can eat all the grass around the pond.

(221) triangle (222) square (223) pentagon (224) hexagon (225) 11 (226) 10 (227) 5 (228) 4 (229) 3 (230) 6 (231) 7 (232) 8 (233) 9 (234) 10 (235) 11 (236) 21 (237) 5 (238) 6 (239) 7 (240) 8 (241) 9 (242) 15 (243) 8 (244) 12 (245) 16 (246) 20 (247) 24 (248) 28 (249) 32 (250) 36 (251) 40 (252) 76 (253) 116 (254) 145 (255) 297 (256) 20 (257) 20 (258) 21 (259) 60

(260) 80

(261)

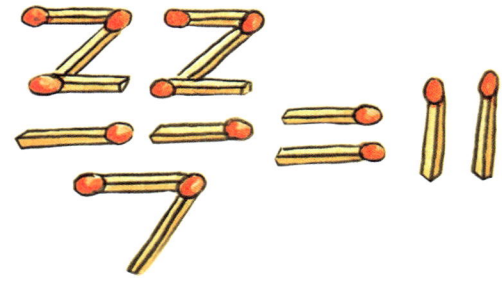

1) $\dfrac{22}{2} = 11$ (reference to the image)

2) $\dfrac{22}{2} \neq 11$ (reference to the image)

3) Place a matchstick to the left of the equals sign.
   (Because there will be 11 matchsticks on the left side, satisfying the equation.)

4) $\dfrac{22}{7} \leq 11$ (reference to the image)

5) $\dfrac{22}{7} \leq \pi\,(3.14)$ (reference to the image)

A Magical Fairytale for
All Elementary School Students

The Rise of a Math Genius

Written by Anho Jo
Published by Lauren Seong

1판 1쇄 발행 2024년 4월 5일

Thanks to:
Translator Yerim An
Illustrator Gukseon Lee
Proofreader Lauren Seong/Gyeongsu Hong

Thanks to:
Storywriter Younghee Hwang
Design Studio Pupcy/Nahyun Kim

Published at POLIVERSE
Publishing registration October 8, 2021 - 000050호
Phone contact (042)639-7749
Homepage www.joanholab.com
E-mail joanhocrew@gmail.com

ISBN 979-11-976207-4-4(73410)

It is a work protected under the copyright law of this book, so unauthorized premise and unauthorized reproduction are prohibited. To use all or part of this book, you must obtain written consent from the copyright holder and Poliverse Co., Ltd. The price of the book is on the back cover.

Book Publishing Poliverse creates a path to knowledge and wisdom for growing teenagers. The future isn't 'universe,' but poliverse!